FAST PHILOSOPHY

Whizz to wisdom in 100 short, funny mental workouts.

ADAM FLETCHER
LUKAS N.P. EGGER

INAUGURATION

A Note from the Authors

Welcome, students.

Today is your first day at *Fast* Philosophy School. Looking around, you may notice that your classroom doesn't look like those in which you've previously studied—perhaps you're stuck in a traffic jam, riding a rickety train to work, or sitting atop a porcelain throne, an unwelcome smell lingering in the air. Don't worry, for this is deliberate.

Did you know that over your lifetime you'll spend more than a year commuting? Two hundred days exercising? A year and a half in the bathroom?! So much of life is comprised of these things: in-between things; on-the-way things; routine things.

What if we could put all that lost time to use? This is the noble goal of *Fast Philosophy*, which provides short, sharp bursts of knowledge. Accordingly, all the content in this book is divided into one hundred bite-sized, entertaining "seatings", perfectly timed for whenever you find yourself with a few minutes to spare and a thirst for enlightenment.

Why study philosophy, you might ask? Isn't it just long-dead Greek and German dudes sitting around pondering their mortality?

Yes. No. *Yeno.* It's complicated, and, like most things, best expressed with a story.

A young philosopher falls madly in love with a young lady, but she isn't interested and rebukes his advances. Like many philosophers, he is best with his pen and decides to write her a love letter every day for a year. She will feel differently about him, surely, if only she understands him better. She will certainly be won over by his dedication and sweet words. For a full year, every day, he sends her that love letter, and she finally agrees to marry . . . *the postman.*

Philosophy: fantastic at identifying problems, noble in its intentions, useful in devising solutions, bad at execution (but often resulting in one for the heretic). Studying philosophy to better understand yourself is like becoming an archbishop to meet girls. That's because it concerns itself only with the questions worth asking—the kinds of questions for which, sadly, there are no easy answers. It's the difference between "What shall I eat for lunch?" and "Is it okay to kill animals in order to eat this delicious bacon cheeseburger for lunch?"

But philosophy matters because it's the study of how to learn. Accordingly, it's the foundation upon which a lifetime of intellectual development can be built. Don't think of it as the pursuit of answers but the quest for better questions. As Einstein said, "We cannot solve our problems with the same thinking we used when we created them." We must create new perspectives (or google furiously).

It's always better to have a question you can't answer than an answer you can't question. Philosophy cannot offer solutions, nor should it. Instead it offers new perspectives and an understanding of what you buy into when adopting one perspective over another.

You now have the honour of trying on the perspectives of some of the most brilliant thinkers of all time.

Your professors, Adam and Lukas

PS: To check that you've been paying attention, we've included a thirty-question graduation test at the end of this book. Pass it and you have the right to tell the world you're an official *Fast Philosopher!*

TL;DR: Each seating ends with a "too long; didn't read" summary. But since this book is pretty much a giant TL;DR of Western philosophy already, there's no excuse for reading only a summary of a summary.

What Is Philosophy Not?

What kind of thinking falls under the umbrella of philosophy as opposed to other (usually better-paid) schools of thought?

Correct, possible, simple—for most questions, it's a matter of picking two out of three answers. If you can't find an answer, yet you still stubbornly care about the question, rejoice! You've found philosophy.

MythBusters: The Philosophy Edition

Ever since prehistoric humans first pointed at the sun and said "ugg", we've been busy attempting to understand the strange world we're born into. In the beginning, we mostly did this through simple variations on the same basic story:

Nothing — God — Funny story of origin (can include unicorns, dragons, monsters, floods, demigods, etc.) — Us (and our superiority over all other living creatures).

These were nice, convenient stories, albeit often random and illogical. Still, they took the pressure off us to solve things. God or other myths had our backs. Even weird occurrences such as war, famine, politics, and chocolate fondue were explainable. Everything was part of a larger, mystical Plan of Higher Meaning, and most of the time even included a scandalous affair or captivating intrigue between gods and unlucky humans.

Believing in these things was fun for a while, but despite the explanations offered by these stories, life stayed random and chaotic. Over time, some people lost faith in their local version of the Plan of Higher Meaning. Maybe because they enjoyed being contrarians. Maybe because the plan seemed too convenient. Maybe because they just really didn't understand the point of chocolate fondue.

About two-and-a-half-thousand years ago these stubborn, cynical people professionalised. They began meeting regularly and publishing their (often heretical) theories on bits of dead tree. They led a gradual shift away from myths as a way to explain the world towards Logos (reasoned discourse). Instead of believing every time God had a bad day we got lightning, or that if we didn't sacrifice enough goats or slaves a mythical sea creature would punish us with a bad harvest, we looked for more rational scapegoats: electrostatic energy; inadequate irrigation; gypsy curses; Monsanto.

These new theories weren't always right either, but at least now we were looking for causality in our world. Input. Output. Cause. Effect. Rinse. Repeat.

Suddenly there was a lot to think about. Since merchants, soldiers, and farmers already had demanding professions of actual value, it was agreed that people without useful skills would get the job of professional thinker. These people would oversee questions about the following:

- **Epistemology:** What can we know about the world? *What can we pretend we know for profit?*
- **Metaphysics:** Why is there anything at all? *Why isn't there more cake?*
- **Ethics:** What does it mean to be good? *How can I get away with not being it?*
- **Aesthetics**: What is beauty? *How can I convince it to have sex with me?*

We called them *philosophers*. You are about to become one!

TL;DR: Despite what you see at the average family party, political rally, or Internet comments section, human society has slowly transitioned from myths (ad hoc explanations) to Logos (reasoned discourse). Philosophers do much discourse but very little disco.

0. **Brain:** Both your best friend and your worst enemy.

1. **Glasses:** A philosopher without glasses (even one with 20/20 vision) is like a swimming pool without water: possible but pointless.

2. **Beard:** See *Glasses*. Beards give you instant intellectual heft. If you're a woman, consider wearing a fake beard.

3. **Mouth:** For saying things like "Strictly speaking, I think what you propose isn't a topic of meta-semantics but rather meta-meta-semantics." Remember, good arguments have three things—coherence, completeness, and ~~correctness~~ jokes.

4. **Relaxed pompousness:** To be a philosopher is to make peace with the contradiction that what you do is both important and will be completely ignored by 99 percent of humanity.

5. **Notepad:** For brilliant thoughts (almost never), clever thoughts (seldomly), inane thoughts (occasionally), and shopping lists (daily).

6. **Virginity:** Optional. But likely to bond you to other philosophers.

7. **Satchel:** For carrying around what you want to read (*Vogue*, *Fifty Shades of Bondage*, *Fast Philosophy*) hidden inside a serious, boring, long-dead philosopher's book with a title like *Summa Theologica*.

8. **Legs:** For folding around a chair while you sit and for running away when people try to set you on fire for being a heretic.

9. **The Sock-ratic method:** Question everything, all the time (more on this in the next seatings). The more uncomfortable this makes people, the more likely you're close to a major breakthrough.

CHAPTER 1

QUESTIONS AND ANSWERS

Why are clouds fluffy?

WHY AREN'T BLUEBERRIES BLUE?

Why do pirates have peg legs?

Why don't infants enjoy infancy as much as adults enjoy adultery?

Why does the tooth fairy want to buy my teeth?

Why doesn't getting 'scared half to death' twice mean you die?

WHY AREN'T WE THERE YET?

SHUT UP.

SEATING
4

The Wisdom of Naiveté

Little Sarah asks her dad, "What is society?"

"Well, my dear," her dad replies, "that's a hard question. Let me try to explain it this way. I'm the breadwinner of the family, so let's call me Capitalism. Mommy is the administrator of the money and in charge, so we'll call her the Government. We're here to take care of your needs, so we'll call you the People. The nanny, well, consider her the Working Class. Your baby brother, we'll call him the Future. Now go think about this and see if it makes sense."

Sarah goes off to bed thinking about what her dad has said. Later that night, she hears her baby brother crying and runs to his room to find that his nappy is soiled. She goes to her parents' room. Her dad is missing. Her mom is sound asleep. Not wanting to wake her, she goes to the nanny's room. Finding the door locked, she looks through the peephole and sees her father in bed with the nanny.

The next morning, Sarah says, "Dad, I think I understand what politics is now."

Her dad looks up from his cereal. "Good, my love. So why don't you explain it to me?"

"Well, Capitalism is screwing the Working Class while the Government is sound asleep, the People are bored and being ignored, and the Future is in deep shit."

Children. Magical, aren't they? Always there to ask why glue doesn't stick inside the tube, or how the sun works, or why penguins don't get cold feet standing on the ice all day without shoes. Their unquenchable thirst for knowledge can sure leave your throat dry and your voice hoarse.

But what if their questioning isn't about them? What if it's really a selfless act on their part to help you understand how little you know? How many of your ideas are incorrect? How many of your assumptions are untested? In many ways, their "question everything to death then question it a few times more to be sure" style of questioning apes that of one of philosophy's greatest minds (and worst dressers): Socrates.

TL;DR: Asking questions is easier than answering them, isn't it? See what we did there? Just when you think you've figured out something, that's the exact moment you'll either be proven wrong or run over by a monster truck.

"Just One More Question, Socrates"

People often think they know things, and it's by questioning these people in a perfectly innocent way that we can reveal to them they do not. While not knowing often feels shameful to us, the philosopher Socrates didn't see it this way. He once said, "I know that I am intelligent, because I know that I know nothing." He even developed a Lieutenant Columbo–like technique for questioning people: the Socratic method.

It's a technique in which the teacher doesn't give information but merely asks a series of questions directing students to the answer, or to a deeper awareness of the limits of their own knowledge. The modern equivalent is probably "show, don't tell". Here's how the method works.

1. Find a statement that sums up the argument. "So you're saying that a sandwich is any food wrapped in bread?""Yes."

2. "Ah." Closely examine the implications of the statement; look for exceptions and loopholes. "What about when what's wrapped is a sausage?"

3. Let the other person try to reason or weasel their way out. "Um, then we call it a hot dog. I guess that's an exception."

4. "Right." Repeat these steps, one challenging, loophole of a question at a time. "And what about when it's a meat patty?"

"Erm. Yes, I guess that's another exception. Then we call it a burger."

"Okay. Wait. Aren't lasagne sheets made from wheat, just like bread?

"Yeah."

"Oh. So, you're also saying lasagne is a sandwich?"

Repeat until you come to the point where your opponent contradicts their initial argument, sighs a lot, and admits that the argument never made any sense (or jumps off the nearest bridge). "Look, man, I just call it a sandwich because . . . Hey, wait, did you secretly eat my lunch?"

5. Appear puzzled and harmless, as if you've done nothing to make the person look stupid. If that doesn't help defuse the situation, run away (see item 8 in the Philosopher's Starter Kit).

Being on the receiving end of this technique is about as enjoyable as toasting your own hand, especially when the teacher is only feigning ignorance, as was often the case with Socrates. But the method's goal is noble: lead the student away from incorrect assumptions and towards truth. Not that it ever led Socrates away from trouble. He was forever scrapping with other philosophers because his method made them look foolish.

TL;DR: It's easy to confuse opinions with facts (and that's an ~~opinion~~ fact). The Socratic method is a simple questioning technique for teasing out people's assumptions. If that fails, it also does a wonderful job of antagonising them.

Philosophy in Diagrams Pt.1

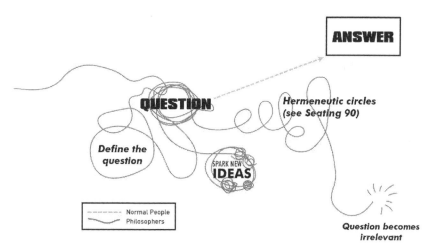

ANSWER

QUESTION

Hermeneutic circles (see Seating 90)

Define the question

SPARK NEW IDEAS

Normal People
Philosophers

Question becomes irrelevant

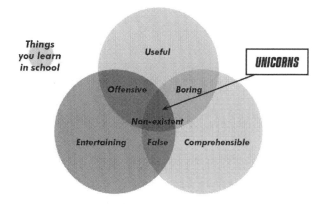

Things you learn in school

Useful

UNICORNS

Offensive   *Boring*

Non-existent

Entertaining   *False*   *Comprehensible*

TL;DR: The fastest way to get from question to solution is a straight answer, unless you're a philosopher, in which case, you prefer to take the scenic route to nowhere. Good answers are like unicorns—mythical.

Fact File: Socrates

Influence: 9/10

Nationality: Greek

Dates: 469 BC – 399 BC

Groupies: Plato, Aristotle, Xenophon, children, TV-chat-show interviewers

· Sōkrátēs ·

Bio: Socrates trained as a stonemason before abandoning (stonewalling?) his profession to roam the streets of Athens teaching/offending people with seemingly innocent questions. He did this so success-fully that he was eventually charged with impiety and corrupting the youth. He would probably have gotten away with your standard exiling had he not had the audacity to answer "free food for life" when asked what he thought would be a fair punishment for his crime. He was promptly served a death sentence.

Worst Idea: Marry your enemy. Socrates had some rather uncon-ventional ideas about love that bordered on the masochistic. His wife, Xanthippe, was a spirited character who is said to have poured a full chamber pot over his head during an argument. He suppos-edly said, "I know full well, if I can tolerate her spirit, I can with ease attach myself to every human being else." This doesn't exactly paint pictures of marital bliss and quiet nights of spooning. (More like chopping one of your arms off so that you can become a really good one-armed juggler.)

Anecdote: Socrates is often depicted as a shabby-vagabond-intellectual-superhero type; someone immune to tiredness, warmth, cold, and the intoxicating effects of alcohol. "No human being has ever seen Socrates drunk," said his friend and pupil Alcibiades. Even in prison, awaiting his death sentence, he was chipper and accepting. When Socrates raised the cup of hemlock to his mouth, a tearful Xanthippe screamed about the atrocity of his dying innocent. Socrates looked at her and replied skittishly, "Do you think it would be better for me if I were guilty?"

Quotes:

"It is not living that matters, but living rightly." *And not winning that matters but winning bigly.*

"Wisdom begins in wonder." *But often ends in indifference, disillusionment, and court.*

"The hottest love has the coldest end." *But the coldest love has the hottest adultery.*

Socrates in Objects:

1. Cane: He often walked around with a stick to intimidate people.

2. Hemlock jug: It's with this poison (and humour) that he met his end.

3. Full chamber pot: Something once poured over his head (although he probably deserved it).

4. Low fixtures and fittings: Socrates was short and stocky (he also had bulging eyes and a snub nose).

5. Stone: His career path was set in stone before he swapped to chiselling other peoples' minds.

6. Spear: While it's hard to imagine (given that he was more the questioner than the follower), Socrates served as a hoplite (foot soldier) for three campaigns.

7. Question-mark poster: The extent to which he liked questions is unquestionable.

8. Pop-culture equivalent: Columbo. Both were short, shabby in dress, and dishevelled in appearance but made up for these things in intellect. One solved crimes, the other died tragically for his.

TL;DR: Socrates was a brilliant philosopher, famous for showing people their prejudices. He would have done so for longer had he not had a prejudice of his own: he believed nothing in life should be taken seriously, not even a charge of corrupting the youth. If they gave out that charge as easily today, there'd be a lot of nervous fast-food sellers, rappers, and YouTube makeup tutorial hosts.

Questioning the Questioner: Ask Socrates

Me? The great Socrates? You want *me* to be an agony aunt and advice columnist? Ironic, since I'm known for saying things like "I cannot teach anybody anything. I can only make them think." But whatever, I'll give it a go. And since I always refuse to take payment for my work, out of principle, I should fit quite well in the poverty machine that is modern-day publishing.

Q: I've been dating my girlfriend for five years, and her family are pressuring me to marry her. Should I? – *Moritz, Stockholm*

A: "By all means, marry. If you get a good wife, you'll become happy; if you get a bad one, you'll become a philosopher." *Get an okay one and you'll probably end up a civil servant.*

Q: Socrates, I panic during exams. Do you have any advice? – *Sandra, Massachusetts*

A: "The unexamined life is not worth living." *But the examined life results in high doctors' fees.*

Q: Socrates, my daughter is a huge Mariah Carey fan and is pestering me to buy concert tickets. Should I? – *Rob, London*

A: "From the deepest desires often come the deadliest hate. There is only one good— knowledge; and only one evil—ignorance." *No, wait, make that two—ignorance and Mariah Carey.*

Q: Socrates! I have a stable boyfriend who drinks less than you, yet I keep thinking about this guy at work. What should I do? – *Susann, LA*

A: "Life contains but two tragedies. One is not to get your heart's desire; the other is to get it." Also, "He who is not contented with what he has, would not be contented with what he would like to have." *So, hmm, tricky. Threesome?*

Q: Hi Socrates, I'm a big fan! I've been employing your Socratic method in my local bar, but with disastrous effects. I've been punched four times, and had a full gin and tonic poured over my head. What am I doing wrong? – *Tim, Montreal*

A: What makes you think you're doing something wrong?

Q: . . . Well, everyone hates me. I try to point out the flaws in their opinions. But they don't want to learn.

A: No one wants to learn. The best way to teach is to not let the other person know he or she is the student.

Q: . . . Okay, but then why does your method have to be so annoying?

A: Well, there's gotta be a little something in it for the teacher, right?

TL;DR: Even though asking Socrates for an answer was like asking a cocker spaniel for accounting advice, he would have made an entertaining agony aunt and advice columnist.

Pimp My Knowing

Why are questions so important? Because answers are easy fodder for those skilled in the dark art of subterfuge. Marketers, politicians, and diplomats are all trained to not give real answers, to mould answers to the expectations of their audience, and to answer the questions they want and not the questions they get. Questions are ladders; answers are snakes.

It's in what we ask that we reveal what we're genuinely interested in. Questions are the starting point for new knowledge. Not all knowledge is the same. In fact, it comes in four distinct categories:

1. **Known knowns.** This is what's traditionally considered knowledge. *I know that I know how old I am, and that I wish my partner were ten years younger.*
2. **Known unknowns.** The category of knowledge Socrates was most proud of. *I know that I don't know the capital of Ecuador.*
3. **Unknown knowns.** Beliefs and superstitions often fall in this category. They're things we either pretend we don't know about or have an untested hypothesis about. *People with symmetrical faces get more dates.*
4. **Unknown unknowns.** True ignorance is not only not knowing but also not knowing what you don't know. They're bits of knowledge you're incapable of acquiring as you weren't even aware they were missing. *I didn't know my*

wife was going to leave me for the milkman. If I had, I'd have gone vegan.

There are also two different ways of knowing:

1. **Knowing that.** Facts. *I shouldn't climb stairs while drunk.*
2. **Knowing how.** Ability. *I know how to call an ambulance after falling down them.*

There's an ongoing debate about whether knowing *how* is more important than knowing *that*, and about whether they're truly distinct or just the same knowledge in slightly different wrapping. (Like how the only difference between most modern art and a landfill is a well-lit room.)

TL;DR: The most dangerous cognitive blind spots are unknown unknowns: things we're unaware we're unaware of. It doesn't matter whether you lack knowing *how* or knowing *that*—when falling down the stairs, it's going to hurt either way.

What Was the Question Again?

Bad things can happen when you're so convinced an answer is correct that you stop checking whether it still fits the question. Think of WALL-E, from the Pixar movie of the same name: the cute little robot tasked with cleaning up earth's trash. He continued choring away even after earth was long abandoned, alone (except for his pet cockroach) with so much trash he'd never be able to complete his task. Still, he remained focused on his battle, oblivious to the fact that the war had been long since lost. At times we as a society, like WALL-E, get so stuck on the answers we've given ourselves that we lose touch with the original questions. The answers become an empty doctrine: unquestionable, sacred, the way things have always been.

This is the big lesson of philosopher E.F. Schumacher's influential book *Small is Beautiful* (we're pretty sure he wasn't referring to bank accounts, IQs, and genitals). In it, he skilfully argues that we made a mistake equating the success of a society with its gross domestic product (GDP). And this mistake has led us to believe GDP growth is unequivocally good. He refers to this belief as gigantism.

For him, gigantism is an example of a runaway answer; a belief that has led us to treat natural resources as expendable income, when really, they're closer to one-off investments. If you look to the natural world, Schumacher explains, you don't find much growth. Instead, you find equilibrium. A balance threatened by gigantism.

To avoid getting stuck with wrong answers, we *Fast* Philosophers must acknowledge two perhaps unintuitive things. Firstly, that an answer can change over time. Growth was good when the human population was two million. Less so at seven billion. Secondly, that an answer depends on its scope. In principle, WALL-E was doing the right thing by cleaning up, but his doing so was futile when applied to the entire globe, after humanity had already left for a life in the stars.

Small is Beautiful attempts to re-evaluate one of our most accepted answers. It also advocates humility in solutions, i.e. taking small risks —while revolution is sexy and overthrowing the system exciting, steady change is usually best. Thus, even if we fail, we can recover. If we bet it all on one answer, one solution, one way, put all our resources on red only to see the ball land on black, it's game over.

This willingness to re-evaluate and challenge the status quo in the face of intimidation, ridicule, and social exile is at the heart of all great philosophy (and dinner-party conversation).

TL;DR: It's dangerous to keep accepting answers long after their questions are invalid. E.F. Schumacher's *Small is Beautiful* challenges society's mantras that "bigger is better" and "growth is good". The continual re-evaluation of answers is at the heart of philosophy. Well, that and tweed.

Philosophy in Diagrams Pt.2

WHAT'S THE PURPOSE OF PHILOSOPHY?

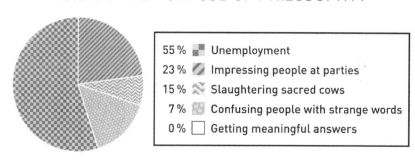

55 % ■ Unemployment
23 % ▨ Impressing people at parties
15 % ≋ Slaughtering sacred cows
7 % ▦ Confusing people with strange words
0 % ☐ Getting meaningful answers

THE VALLEY OF IGNORANCE

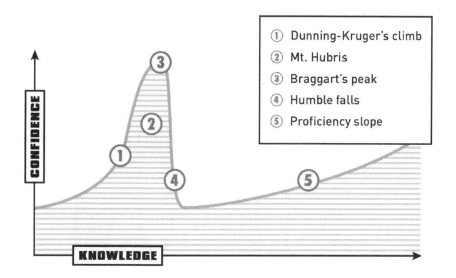

① Dunning-Kruger's climb
② Mt. Hubris
③ Braggart's peak
④ Humble falls
⑤ Proficiency slope

CONFIDENCE

KNOWLEDGE

TL;DR: While it'll do about as much for your career as a face tattoo, philosophy (and gin and tonic) is the best thing to serve to attractive people at parties. The road to knowledge is bumpier than a pickle, on a speed bump, on the moon.

Let It Go – The Truth

Today we laugh at the people who thought the world was flat, or that having their picture taken could steal their soul. We ridicule the things they knew as the laughable beliefs of naive simpletons. So why is it we pretend to have knowledge when we know, rationally, everything we regard today will probably be equally derided by future generations? How has the reputation of truth remained so remarkably unblemished considering its extensive track record of disappointing, publicly embarrassing, and swindling people?

Perhaps truth is such a tantalising elixir because it promises to negate our fundamental human shortcomings: while we are fleeting, it shines eternal; while we are flawed, it is irrefutable; while we are limited, truth is absolute (like the vodka). It's an antidote to the existential fears we face as conscious, mortal beings.

If we can find truth—how something really is, how something really works—not only do we gain order and understanding, but we're also able to transcend our in-built physical limitations and flaws. Faced with our shortcomings, we subconsciously turn them around and start idolising them. Therefore, by worshipping truth, we worship our own flaws in disguise.

It's a neat psychological trick, yet, like alchemy, correct selfie angles, and good excuses for wearing hot pants, truth always eludes us. Other than a few mathematical facts, everything is subject to revision over time, most things more than once. Often the only difference between truth and lies and then truth again is the amount of time that's passed (and the size of the book advance). The surer we were about a particular truth, the more discomfort we feel when it's revealed as just another myth, inherited custom, or cognitive wrong turn.

So, dearest *Fast* Philosopher, try to let go of the ideas of truth, answers, and knowledge; they will only bog you down. Most of the time, people who sell truths are only selling interesting stories in charming packages via monthly subscriptions. Besides, you'll never know how much of what you say, think, or feel is true. And having truth discovered by other people just ruins all the fun. It's like getting to play detective in a crime long solved.

As we advance through the seatings, laugh, ridicule, ponder, think, believe, hypothesise, wonder, and dream but don't let yourself be tricked by pretty little words such as "know" and "truth". Almost everything is better if not taken too seriously*. Truth feels good, but in reality, it's unobtainable. As proven by a little something called Münchhausen's trilemma.

TL;DR: Truth is mostly just an attractive illusion. The truth is that we're better off if we don't take it too seriously. Questions will always be much more interesting than answers. (And celebrity gossip much more interesting than questions.)

*Except marriage proposals, life-and-death situations, and family Monopoly games. Take these things seriously.

The Truth about Münchhausen's Trilemma

Münchhausen's trilemma was conceived by philosopher Hans Albert to explain why no statement can ever be fully proven. When taken to their logical conclusion, all answers and assertions claiming to be truth fall into one of three traps: unsupported assertion, infinite regression, or circular reasoning.

Trap 1 – Unsupported assertion: Also known as dogma. In an unsupported assertion, the premise justifies itself. *X is true because, come on, it's X!* Telltale signs that you've hit rock bottom in your willingness to search for the truth are phrases such as "everyone knows that" and "because it's obvious!" This appeal to "common sense" or "obvious truths" never reveals anything new. It simply ensures that the conversation stops before someone says something no one wants or is allowed to hear. "Everyone knows unicorns taste like caramel. I mean, come on, it's so obvious."

Trap 2 – Infinite regression: The premise lives on forever in the form of other premises. *X will be true once we prove W, and we can prove W if we first prove V, and we can prove V if we first prove U.* "We exist because the universe exists, and the universe exists because God made it exist, and God exists because . . ."

Trap 3 – Circular reasoning: An assertion that references itself as its justification. *X is true because Y, and Y is true because X.* "The Bible is the word of God. God tells us so in the Bible."

The trilemma is named after notorious half-truth merchant Baron Münchhausen. The good baron claimed to have once gotten trapped in a swamp with his horse only to pull himself out by his own hair. In attempting to find answers and irrefutable truths, we're like Münchhausen. There is no neutral place for us to stand while we establish them. No distance we can have from them. We're always sinking in the swamp of our beliefs, trying to pull ourselves out by our own hair.

This probably sounds horrible to you, as though it undermines the fundamental usefulness of philosophy. However, it's not as bad as it seems. As a *Fast* Philosopher, you get to willingly accept the limitations of your subject. You get to swap the fallacy of thinking you know something for the certainty that you won't be tricked into believing something that simply cannot be. Well, unless it's to your advantage to do so (such as with the Tooth Fairy, Santa Claus, or 'Til Death Do Us Part).

TL;DR: Münchausen's trilemma shows that all answers and assertions claiming to be the truth will fall into one of three traps: unsupported assertion, infinite regression, or circular reasoning. Nevertheless, you will encounter many statements that insist they've pulled themselves out of the swamp of incorrectness by their own hair.

CHAPTER 2

TRUTH AND CORRESPONDENCE

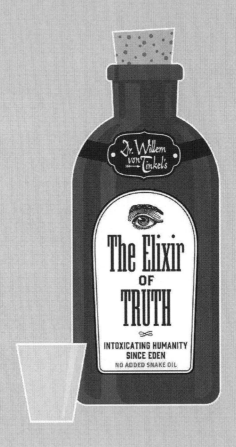

Dr. Willem von Tinkel's

The Elixir
OF
TRUTH

INTOXICATING HUMANITY
SINCE EDEN
NO ADDED SNAKE OIL

SEATING
13

The FOX Cave

Imagine that at birth you were taken away from your loving parents and put into a room with two other babies your age. Your basic needs (water, exercise, diapers, love, and chocolate cake) are not part of this imagined world. You're a very, very low-maintenance human, happy just to sit there.

In the room are a sofa and a television. The television is on twenty-four hours a day, and locked to the TV channel FOX. You call it "ugg", and it's your view to reality. Eighteen years pass like this.

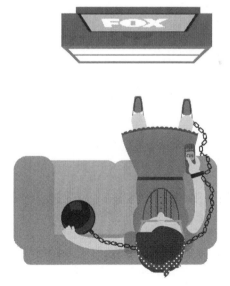

If you'd only ever watched ugg, what do you think you would understand of the world? What would So You Think You Can Dance *and* The F Word *teach you about humanity?*

One day, you manage to escape the room and step gingerly out into the "real world". At first you're completely overwhelmed. But as time goes on, you slowly adjust. You realise the world you thought you were seeing via ugg is television's depiction of the real world. TV shows you just one shade, but there is actually a whole spectrum of humanity.

Should you return and tell your fellow captives what you've learnt? What would you tell them about the world outside this room? How can you explain something to someone if this person lacks the references needed to understand it? Wouldn't it be like describing blue to someone who is blind?

You return to the room. You find your fellow captives as you left them, watching away, seemingly oblivious to the fact that you left. You take your old seat. "That's not a real living room. It's a TV set of a living room!" you say, while watching a chat show.

"What are you talking about?" one of your co-captives replies, his gaze still locked to the screen.

"The real world!" you say, leaping up from your chair.

"This is the real world," says the other, pointing at ugg.

You laugh maniacally. "It's not. It's 2D and barely a shadow of the real world. It's all fake. I've seen the real world."

"Shut up!" shouts the other, standing up to face you. "You're nothing but a liar."

He pushes you, and you fall back into your seat. The threat of violence hangs in the room. You would argue more, but *Survivor* has started. *Eudaimonia*, the pursuit of happiness and human flourishing, is simply powerless against reality TV's drama, intrigue, and highly subjective editing. You sit down to watch.

TL;DR: If you spent your whole life locked in a room with just a television, what knowledge would you have of the real world? Could you understand it? Survive within it? Can you suffer from Stockholm syndrome when you're your own captor? If you do so while in Stockholm, is it Stockholm Stockholm syndrome?

Plato's (Un)Justified True Beliefs

The FOX cave is a modern example of an allegory called Plato's cave. Plato was convinced that beneath our normal world there exists a nonphysical but substantial "ideal" world. In our normal, imperfect world, we're trapped in a cave, not seeing reality but mere shadows cast before us upon its wall—derivatives of the pure, perfect world of forms.

It's only rational thought that allows us to sneak out of this cave and into the real world of pure ideas, he believed. Plato's cave is often seen as the cornerstone of all his philosophy. When he created it, philosophy and the sciences were still in their infancy. There was little to no division between state, religion, and myth. This simple cave metaphor helped Plato to sell the idea of rationality through philosophy. This is why it's so noteworthy.

In his allegory, the sun shines brightly outside the cave (assuming the cave is not in England), representing the idea of the good. This light illuminates the world for what it actually is, offering those smart enough to grasp this idea a chance to escape their personal caves. Free of them, they can then validate assumptions about how the world works, separating them from doctrine and superstition.

How does one escape? Rationality. Plato had a framework for rational knowledge that we now call the justified true belief (JTB) theory: If a claim (C) is true, and believed and justified by (P), we can call it knowledge. Let's break that down.

1. (C) is true. *Obviously this must be the case, as knowledge pertains only to true things.*

2. (P) believes that (C) is true. *You know only what you believe to be true.*

3. (P) is justified in believing that (C) is true. *There have to be good reasons for your conviction, to separate your belief from mere assumption and guesswork.*

Philosophers liked Plato's JTB idea so much that it became the gold standard in philosophy for more than two millennia, bringing light to the dark cave that is our existence without rationality.

TL;DR: Plato felt that all of us live in a cave, and rather than seeing the truth, we watch mere shadows of ideals cast on the wall. The easiest way out of this cave is to ensure our beliefs are true and justified. If that fails, you can always get rich leading people on tours through the darkness.

FAST, HARD, ACTION-PACKED EPISTEMOLOGY! Two innate thumbs up!
Karl M.
Justified T. Belief
in
Hughman Perception
Plato's Cave
IN A WORLD OF SHADOWS, HUMANITY MUST SEE THE LIGHT.
INFLUENCED BY P SOCRATIC THINKER
PRODUCED BY GREE K. SLAVES / MUSIC BY PYTHAGORAS IN ASSOCIATION WITH APOLLO & DIONYSUS INC.
EXPLICIT NAKED TRUTH. ONLY SUITABLE FOR MATURE AUDIENCES (AND PHILOSOPHERS)

Fact File: Plato

Influence: 8/10

Nationality: Greek

Dates: 428 BC – 347 BC

Groupies: Aristotle, Plotinus, St Augustine

· Platón ·

Bio: Plato was the most famous student of Socrates. He was a prolific writer and established his own school, the Academy. Together with his student Aristotle, he laid the groundwork for all Western philosophy. He was so successful that some philosophers quip that all Western philosophy is but a footnote to Plato.

Greatest Idea: The theory of ideas. For him, the "real world" was made from derivative shadows of the real thing. So, a stool is connected to the idea of the perfect stool. That stool, however, is not part of our world but the world of ideas. The world of ideas is not perceptible through senses, as senses can be misleading, but better travelled to by rational thought. Accurate knowledge can only be acquired by rational reason (or significant bribery).

Worst Idea: Plato argued a just state could come into being only if ruled by a philosopher. He almost succeeded in convincing the tyrant of Syracuse, Sicily, to convert to philosophy and rule as a philosopher king. The experiment crashed and burnt prematurely, sending Syracuse into economic decline and invasion.

Anecdote: Plato tried to come up with a definition for "human beings". He theorised that man was best described as an animal without feathers walking on two legs. When Diogenes of Sinope heard about this definition, he immediately went to the market to get a rooster. Having purchased the rooster, he plucked its feathers and yelled triumphantly: "There you have your human, Plato!" But Plato was more a man of principles than humour. He didn't renounce his definition but instead added "and flat nails" to it.

Quotes:

"One of the penalties for refusing to participate in politics is that you end up being governed by your inferiors." *Ninety-five percent of politicians give the other 5 percent a really bad reputation.*

"Wise men talk because they have something to say; fools because they have to say something." *Talk is silver, silence is gold, social media is platinum.*

"Love is a serious mental disease." *Schizophrenia of the loins.*

Plato in Objects:

1. Teacher's cap: In 388 BC, Plato founded his own influential school, the Academy.

2. Travel guides: He travelled a lot.

3. Wrestling singlet: He used to be a wrestler.

4. Money: He was from a wealthy family.

5. Quill: He was also a playwright, considered a major contributor to Greek literature.

6. Pop-culture equivalent: Yoda. Both were recognised by their peers as great, wise minds frequently asked to provide insights and to mentor. Yet neither was exactly clear or concise in his words. Ironi-

cally, Yoda sent Luke into a cave to gain knowledge, while Plato wanted all of us to get out of it to see the world for what it really is.

TL;DR: Plato was a student of Socrates and laid the groundwork for all Western philosophy. He was a bit like Yoda—an influential sage. He wanted us all to come out into the sun, presumably where he intended to get richer by selling us ice cream, suntan lotion, and agoraphobia medication.

The Right Way to Wrong

It's a nice summer's day, and you nip into your local shop to buy ice cream. On your way out, you hear a woman scream. A bearded man in black glasses and a blue T-shirt runs past you. Turning to your right, you see an old woman lying on the street crying hysterically. You rush to help her, as do several other people. She explains that a young man in a blue T-shirt has just stolen her bag.

A minute later, two police vans arrive. Since you saw the robber running away, you describe him to them. "He was young, bearded, had short-cropped hair, a blue T-shirt, and black glasses," you tell them. An officer puts the description out over his radio. You stay to console the woman, and a few minutes later the policeman informs you both that they've arrested someone nearby in a blue T-shirt and black glasses carrying the woman's wallet.

Everyone thanks you. You set off for home feeling like a hero. Then, as you turn into your street, you see the exact same bearded man in a blue T-shirt. Quite the surprise. He should be under arrest, yet here he is, jogging past you, his T-shirt soaked through with sweat.

It takes you a minute to work out what's happened. This is the man you saw earlier as you exited the shop—he wasn't a mugger, just a jogger, out running laps around the neighbourhood. He wasn't running away but simply running! The actual mugger, it turns out, scarpered off in the opposite direction and was out of sight before you stepped out onto the street. You didn't see him. By coincidence, both the jogger and the mugger were wearing blue T-shirts, had beards, and wore black glasses. You didn't know that. You made all the wrong assumptions but got the right answer.

So the question is this: were you right about the mugger's description? Can you be still be considered right about something even if all the reasoning you have for that belief is later proven to be incorrect?

TL;DR: Can you still be said to have gotten the right answer if all your workings are incorrect? How can it be wrong when it feels so right? How fast do you have to be to outrun the truth?

The Gettier Problem

In 1963, American philosopher Edmund Gettier presented a two-and-a-half-page paper that showed, through some clever examples, a fundamental flaw in the justified true belief framework. He displayed that it's possible to believe something, be justified in believing it, and even be right about it and yet still be able to claim that you didn't know anything about it. This is a little complicated, so let's look at that mugging story again using the JTB framework.

1. (C) is true. *The mugger was wearing a blue T-shirt. The old woman said so.*

2. (P) believes that (C) is true. *You believed the mugger was wearing a blue T-shirt, based on her description.*

3. (P) is justified in believing that (C) is true. *The old woman told you the mugger was wearing a blue T-shirt and you saw a person fitting that description running from the scene of the crime.*

Philosophically speaking, your belief meets the JTB criteria. Yet you didn't know anything about the actual mugger—you only knew something about a person who happened to share his features. Examples like this undermined JTB and left philosophers with an important question to answer (or argue endlessly about until everyone got bored): if you get the right answer but for incorrect reasons, are you still technically correct?

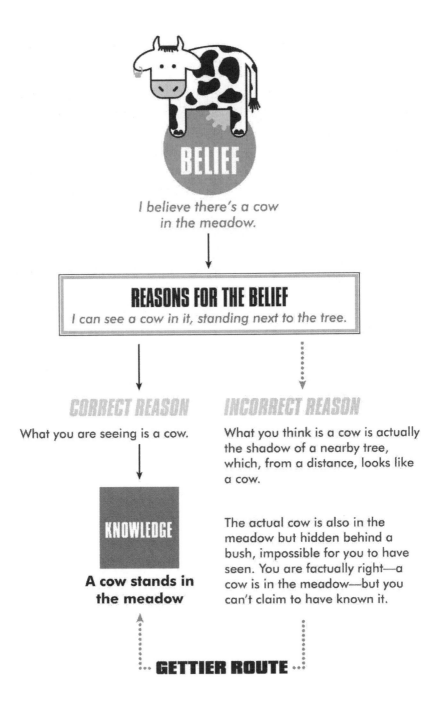

I believe there's a cow
in the meadow.

REASONS FOR THE BELIEF
I can see a cow in it, standing next to the tree.

CORRECT REASON

What you are seeing is a cow.

KNOWLEDGE

**A cow stands in
the meadow**

INCORRECT REASON

What you think is a cow is actually
the shadow of a nearby tree,
which, from a distance, looks like
a cow.

The actual cow is also in the
meadow but hidden behind a
bush, impossible for you to have
seen. You are factually right—a
cow is in the meadow—but you
can't claim to have known it.

GETTIER ROUTE

Many philosophers would have admitted, through gritted teeth, that you were right. Even though you were right in the same sense that a broken clock still shows the correct time twice a day.

With JTB undermined, many rushed to try to prove Gettier wrong and develop a new model for knowledge to replace JTB. However, the proposed fixes haven't been universally accepted, so no new model has been established. As a result, a lot of philosophers have developed selective amnesia regarding Gettier and, like cartoon characters running off a cliff, simply continue as if everything is fine as long as no one acknowledges the problem exists.

TL;DR: The Gettier problem undermined the usefulness of the justified true belief framework. It showed you can end up with a correct claim even if the reasons you believe in it are incorrect. Consequently, arriving at a right claim has gotten easier, since philosophy has agreed (somewhat) that you can now take a scenic detour there via wrong beliefs. If you regularly get lost on your way to truth, consider investing in a new (mental) map.

The Truth and Wisdom of Being Almost the Same Thing

"Truth" is often used interchangeably with "knowledge" and "wisdom". However, there's a fine line between these concepts. Truth is abstract, knowledge is personal, and wisdom is the shell surrounding them both. Consider the following.

There's truth in knowing that a tomato is a fruit. There's wisdom in not putting it in a fruit salad.

There's truth in knowing that the Internet holds the answer to just about everything. There's wisdom in knowing that you'll not find it on Facebook.

There's truth in knowing that your partner said, "It's fine." There's wisdom in knowing that it's anything but "fine".

TRUTH
Pigs are cute.

WISDOM
I don't want any knowledge about how sausages are made.

There's truth in knowing that humans share more than 95 percent of their genes with monkeys. There's wisdom in knowing it's a bad idea to throw your shit at people.

There's truth in knowing that the cake tastes good. There's wisdom in knowing that diabetes is a serious illness.

There's truth in knowing that carrots contain vitamin A and could potentially help you see in the dark. There's wisdom in not trying to use them like torches.

There's truth in knowing you ticked the box marked "I read the terms and conditions". There's wisdom in knowing that the only thing you know about the terms and conditions is that they come with a box.

There's truth in knowing you have 867 friends on Facebook. There's wisdom in knowing there are only twelve people in the world who would lend you twenty dollars.

There's truth in knowing that the item is reduced by 50 percent. There's wisdom in knowing it's still double the price it should be.

There's truth in knowing that the cinema is only 50 percent full. There's wisdom in knowing there's a 99 percent chance an extraordinarily tall person is going to come and sit in front of you.

TL;DR: Truth and knowledge are not the same, but wisdom can reconcile the differences. It's the difference between being able to identify shit and having the wisdom to know when you're being a shit.

Terms and Conditions of Truth

Explaining what makes a proposition true should be easy, right? Something is true if it's a fact, a reality, an undisputable. But consider the statement "leprechauns are small". Is this true because it represents the world accurately? Or simply because we've all agreed leprechauns are vertically challenged? What if we didn't agree? How can we ever know which of the many thoughts swirling around in our brains are accurate?

The four most important theories about truth are:

1. Correspondence Theory of Truth: It's true because reality confirms it. For example, "All Phil Collins fans are deaf" is true if we don't meet a Phil Collins fan with functioning hearing (unlikely).

Advantages: We can observe and measure the world.

Disadvantages: Those observations are subjective and require interpretation. How can we know if we've found all Phil Collins fan(s). How are we defining "fan" and "deaf"?

2. Coherence Theory of Truth: It's true because of other truths. For example, "The galactic ruler Xenu brought souls to earth" is true because it says so in the book *Operating Thetan Level III*, which is true because OT III scientologists told me it was, which is true because L. Ron Hubbard wrote it, which is true because I paid a lot of money to get that information.

Advantages: You don't have to reconcile everything with everything else.

Disadvantages: Your truth depends on other truths, which might only be valid in a few instances.

3. Pragmatic Theory of Truth: It's true because I want it to be true. For example, "What happens in Vegas stays in Vegas" is true if what happens in Vegas really does stay in Vegas and doesn't sue you for child-support money.

Advantages: Practical. Truth is psychological; you are its guardian.

Disadvantages: Truth is relative, and not independently verifiable.

4. Semantic Theory of Truth: It's true because language makes it so. For example, German Chancellor Gerhard Schröder said that Putin was a "flawless democrat". This is true if we accept that by "flawless" he meant "highly flawed" and that by "democrat" he meant a person with enough oil money/KGB connections to make you go "missing", and by "missing" we mean the no-longer-breathing type of missing.

Advantages: Our language can assign truth value to things.

Disadvantages: Our language is as artificial as a yellow rubber duck in cling film.

TL;DR: There are many theories about how something can be called true—correspondence, coherence, pragmatism, semantics, etc. If you find that sufficiently confusing, don't sweat it. Philosophers are confused as well. Truth doesn't come with usage instructions, terms and conditions, or a refund policy. As with one-armed bandits, second-hand cars, and three-legged horses, it's a case of buyer beware.

Of All the Things I've Lost, I Miss Truth the Most

Rather than thinking of truth as something that can be had like a possession, a physical thing, we must think of it as closer to a doing, an act, a statement of intent (e.g. marketers are regularly "doing" truth).

THE ONTOLOGY OF TRUTH

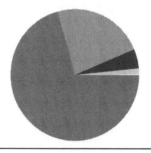

74 %	Things we will probably never know we don't know.
24 %	Things we know we don't know.
4 %	Things we know but will be proven hilariously wrong.
0.6 %	Things we accurately know.
0.005 %	Things the fortune cookie knows.
0.001 %	Things your telephone psychic knows.

THE SPECTRUM OF TRUTH

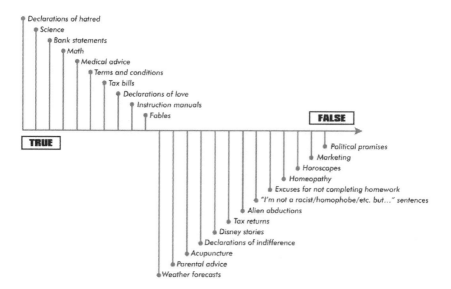

TL;DR: Truth is hard to pin down, and most PR people, magicians, and fortune tellers base their careers on not wrestling it. Do as André Gide said, "trust those who seek the truth, doubt those who say they've found it."

CHAPTER 3

BEING AND PURPOSE

THE MEANING OF LIFE

IS YOUR LIFE LACKING BEING AND PURPOSE? DO YOU HAVE DIFFICULTY JUSTIFYING YOUR (MOSTLY POINTLESS) EXISTENCE? THEN TAKE A FREE PURPOSE...

TINDER · CHOCOLATE · SEX · CHOCOLATE+SEX · INSTAGRAM · BEER & SPORTS · KITTENS · PROCRASTINATION · MIDDLE MANAGEMENT · BECOMING WEALTHY

Otto the VW Bus

Imagine that five years ago you purchased a beautiful midnight-blue VW bus from a long-haired hippie called George, that you met at a music festival. It was a 1974 limited edition, modified to include a pull-out double bed and a home cinema system. It was love at first sight. Over the years you and Otto travelled everywhere together. You climbed mountains, you parked on sandy beaches, and each night, you lay in bed, looked up through Otto's skylight at a star-filled sky, and felt truly happy (and often quite drunk because you added that mini beer fridge).

Since Otto was quite an old, somewhat doddery friend, at the end of every trip you'd repair him, swapping out his old parts for new.

One day, while looking over at the pile of spare parts that you kept, you realise, to your amazement, that you've replaced every single part of Otto. The only original thing that remains is the tatty, fluffy red dice hanging from the rear-view mirror. Which gets you thinking.

If all the parts are new, is the vehicle in front of you still Otto? If it isn't, then at what point did the vehicle stop being your old friend? When 50 percent of the parts had been replaced? Or 66 percent? Or 99 percent?

Yes, you decide, it's still him. His individual parts don't matter.

Then you have an idea. You could take all those spare parts and assemble another VW bus. But this would raise different questions.

If Otto is in front of you, what would this new-old VW bus be? Would this be the real Otto? Can there be two?

This problem was known to the Greeks two thousand years ago; the same thing happened to a ship belonging to a guy called Theseus (ultimately a compliment to spare-part availability and pricing in Greco-Roman times).

If you want a less abstract, pop-culture version of this conundrum, consider the Sugababes paradox. The Sugababes were a British music trio popular in the early 2000s. Every original member left the band at some point and was replaced by a new girl. By the end, they were still called the Sugababes, but the band had none of the original members. Then the original three members of the Sugababes settled their differences and reunited under a different name. So the question is, who are the real Sugababes (and since they haven't had a hit song in ten years, why should anyone care)?

TL;DR: If you replace something part by part, can you still say that the original thing exists? And perhaps more importantly, why do those spare parts always end up costing more than the original whole?

Everything Flows (Even Girl Groups)

The ship of Theseus brain-teaser dates back to an argument between Plutarch and Heraclitus, which lead to a further argument, not about ships, but about rivers. As the water in a river is always changing, when you return to dip your toes, can it be said to still be the same river? Can you walk in the same river twice?

Decide now and let's see how our answer fits other philosophers.

If you think the river is still the same thing: You're like Greek philosopher Heraclitus, who felt that while the flow of water changes, and time passes, the river *itself* remains: "There is nothing permanent except change."

If you think the river becomes something new: You're like Greek philosopher Plutarch, who was obviously attached to his Otto and said it cannot be the same river because the river itself "scatters and again comes together, and approaches and recedes".

If you think it's something in between: You're a cop-out. But Aristotle was with you. He believed a thing is not just one thing, one object, but that that object is made up of many "causes".

1. The material cause = Otto's raw materials

2. The formal cause = the form which makes up Otto

3. The efficient cause = the process followed to combine the parts into Otto

4. The final cause = Otto's actual purpose (providing you with mobile hedonism)

You might have slowly changed Otto's material cause but nothing else.

TL;DR: There is contention as to how many times you can step into the same river. The only thing we know for sure is you'll keep getting wet and so should dress appropriately.

Fact File: Aristotle

Influence: 9/10

Nationality: Greek

Dates: 384 BC – 322 BC

Groupies: Everyone (often referred to simply as "the Philosopher")

· Aristotélēs ·

Bio: Aristotle was one of those annoying people who makes everything look easy. A prolific thinker and writer, he contributed to almost all popular Greek fields of study— logic, political philosophy, rhetoric, epistemics, and ethics.

Greatest Idea: Syllogisms. Aristotle was one of the first to understand the power of logic. By grouping things, you can define what makes them what they are, and so better analyse them. Rather than seeing the world as a giant pile of things, you break them down systematically. You create rules for them. For example, animals can be sorted into mammals, birds, fish, reptiles, amphibians, and invertebrates. This kind of reasoning led Aristotle to create syllogisms: if all As are Bs, and B is a C, then A is also a C. If Keanu Reeves (A) is a man (B), and all men fart (C), Keanu Reeves (A) farts (C). Believe it or not, this was one of the first formal systems of logic ever devised.

Worst Idea: The head is a radiator. He believed that humans are more rational than animals mainly because our blood is better tempered. The main organ responsible for cooling humans' hot-bloodedness, in his view, is the brain. The whole head is largely a radiator venting excess heat, and so to Aristotle, having a runny nose was a clear sign of leakage. It's not known if the phrase "keep a cool head" originates from this era, but as ridiculous as his radiator idea sounds today, it was a seriously discussed and argued theory at that time.

Anecdote: A travelling philosopher was giving a presentation in front of Aristotle. Unfortunately, the presentation didn't kindle any flames of interest, and after an hour of listening to the bland monologue, Aristotle dozed off. The guest realised and asked the great philosopher in an offended tone, "Do you have to sleep whilst I am speaking?" Aristotle replied, "No, not at all. I do it absolutely voluntarily!"

Quotes:

"We are what we repeatedly do . . ." *Most of us are a mixture of nothing, Internet pornography, and biscuits.*

". . . Excellence, then, is not an act, but a habit." *If habits are repeated actions and actions are manifested convictions and convictions just accumulated thought, why can't we just think our way to excellency?*

"It is the mark of an educated mind to be able to entertain a thought without accepting it." *It is the mark of a philosopher's mind to be able to accept it but in no way entertain anyone with it.*

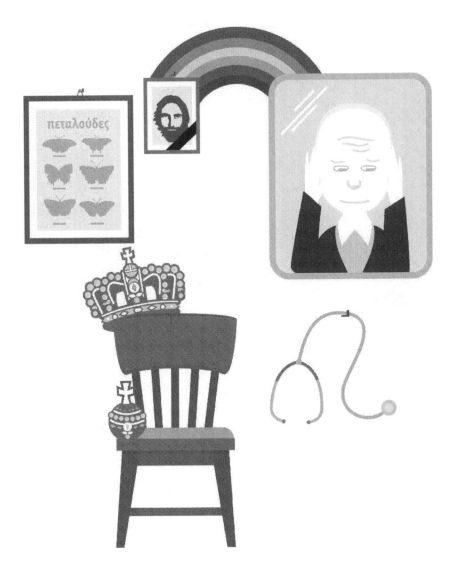

Aristotle in Objects:

1. Royal insignia: King Philip from Macedonia invited Aristotle to teach his son Alexander, who would later become Alexander the Great.

2. Butterfly collection: Aristotle travelled to the island of Lesbos and researched zoology.

3. Arabic book: It's believed that only one-third of his writings survived, and it's only thanks to Muslim scientists that we have any of them.

4. Nicomachus photograph: His son Nicomachus died at a young age in battle.

5. Stethoscope: He belonged to a noble family and his father was a doctor.

6. Rainbow: He had a homoerotic affair with a young student named Palaephatus of Abydus.

7. Pop-culture equivalent: Professor Charles Xavier. Both extremely gifted, they excelled at everything they turned their gigantic intellect to. Both founded their own schools and had to deal with their students going rogue. Aristotle had a young student called Alexander, a nobleman's son, who finished his education and set out on a conquest to take over the entire known world. He managed it, earning himself the grander title "Alexander the Great". Aristotle accompanied him during many of his exploits.

TL;DR: Aristotle was a hugely prolific Greek philosopher who greatly advanced all the areas of knowledge in which he worked. Excluding radiators.

The Great Chain of Being

In the Middle Ages, scholars were obsessed with ranking things. They wanted to show that there was a strict hierarchical structure to all matter and life. Aristotle created such a ladder, called the ladder of nature. Christian scholars took his idea but found one thing lacking: he'd not placed anything above humankind. So scholastic scholars gave God a special position floating ephemerally above the ladder, like a benevolent cloud. This system of classification became known as the Great Chain of Being.

It's a simple system. As rocks haven't unionised, they can't complain and must settle for mere existence on the bottom. No other perks. As you move up the hierarchy, each subdivision coincides with more positive attributes while retaining those of the steps beneath. Plants not only get existence, but life as well. Animals get motion and appetite, which leads us to humankind, which gets all of that plus spa weekends.

The great
CHAIN
of being

While it's appealing to see nature as one united concept, especially if you're at the top, the big problem with the ladder is that you're not allowed to skip positions. You are, for better or worse, stuck, especially if you're a rock. This might explain why Charles Darwin's theory of evolution wasn't a runaway success when it was first introduced; it contradicted the chain's premise of discrete and immutable stages of existence, offering only the much wobblier selective pressure and survival of the fittest, which collapsed the ladder, leaving everyone (and their selfish genes) scrapping in a big heap of natural selection.

Surprisingly, Aristotle's concept still resonates today, probably because we still fancy ourselves as being on top, despite no tree ever having waged a world war, needed a Great Wall, or invented a boy band.

TL;DR: People used to believe that there was an unchanging hierarchical structure of existence. If you want to be on top of the ladder, unionise, and don't be a rock.

Finding Your Purposelessness

Building on the classification work of Aristotle and the Ancient Greeks, medieval monks further developed the ladder of nature. The monks were convinced that every living thing has a purpose; a function to perform in the circle of life, from the plants making oxygen to the wildebeests becoming the lion's lunch. Which leaves us.

If everything else has a purpose, what is ours? Why are we here? If nothing matters, why do anything? If everything matters, what do we do first? How can we live a purposeful life?

For Italian philosopher Giovanni Pico della Mirandola, the answer was simple: the monks were wrong; we have no purpose. We are the only beings freed of a clear-cut, prescriptive destiny. Unlike rocks, plants, and dolphins, we get to decide what's worthy of our time. We can collect stamps, we can stamp on ants, we can climb a mountain, or we can climb into bed. All are equally worthy. Which is both liberating and intimidating at the same time.

For Mirandola, being able to choose your own purpose and destiny was the ultimate source of dignity. Just as God can choose to create anything, so can we, within the framework of our lives. We're free to spend our time however we want. He felt that this made us divine.

So, the next time your partner comes into the room to find you with your feet up on the coffee table, staring out of the window, and asks what you're doing (and why it's not the laundry), simply answer "nothing" and smile. For our friend Mirandola believed you have no purpose, and that's just fine.

TL;DR: According to philosopher Giovanni Pico della Mirandola, humans are the only living thing without a purpose. This makes us divine yet useless. Like candy floss.

Where Do Personalities Come From? (Hint: Not Storks)

If we, as humans, have no innate purpose, what is it that makes us decide one path over another? Why do some of us become jugglers or internationally renowned philanderers while others are happy with their steady, plodding jobs as insurance salespeople?

For most people, the answer is obvious. Allowing for a little chance and serendipity, we become who we are because of our personalities. And in those we are greatly varied; some of us would sell our own grandmother for five minutes in front of the camera while others shun the limelight and fear public speaking more than death.

Which leads us to our next questions: Where do our personalities come from? And why are we so different? Here's an overview of some of the many theories.

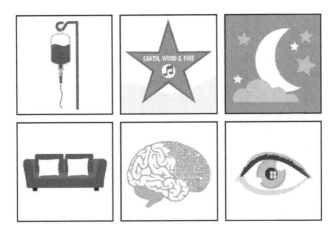

1. Our body fluid. The Egyptians first popularised the idea of a connection between the four temperaments (sanguine, choleric, melancholic, and phlegmatic) with the four bodily fluids (blood, yellow bile, black bile, and phlegm). The balance of these fluids was held accountable for our mood. Incidentally, the word "temperament" comes from the Latin word for "correct mixture" (if you want to see the dangers of incorrect mixtures, take a trip to any dive bar on a Friday night).

2. The elements. Greek philosophers took that four-part Egyptian blood cocktail but poured it over some more relatable elements:

- Sanguine (air): optimistic and leader-like

- Choleric (fire): bad-tempered and irritable

- Melancholic (earth): analytical and quiet

- Phlegmatic (water): relaxed and peaceful

While these might seem random, they're significantly less esoteric (and easier to memorise) than the Myers-Briggs system.

3. The stars. Astrology remains an all-time favourite way to explain deviant desires and absurd attitudes. It says that the alignment of the planets and stars at our birth decides our personality, which is then further affected by celestial movements. You've probably met a few work colleagues who are in desperate need of a celestial realignment and that you hope might disappear into a black hole.

4. Our parents. Mr Freud and his couch felt pretty sure our personalities were mostly nurture, not nature. The advantage in this theory is that we get to blame everything on our parents! Yay!

5. Brain wiring. Neuroscience says it's nature, not nurture, stupid. The wiring (or miswiring) of your brain and its various chemical processes decides whether you're as cool as a cucumber or as fiery as a flamingo. Yes, flamingos are fiery. No, I'm not just projecting based on a personal childhood trauma at a wildlife park. No, I didn't start it. He did. No, I don't want to talk about it.

6. The soul. Theology prefers the idea that the soul is the root of our personality. Where is the soul located? Why do our personalities change when the soul gets hungry/horny? *Shhh.*

The reason there are so many different, wacky theories, each with their own zealous advocates, is probably because of the Barnum effect (aka the Forer effect): people are more likely to believe in things that validate their own world view. Geminis believe more strongly in astrology when it tells them they're highly creative than when it accuses them of being narcissistic. In short, it's always easiest to make money by telling people things they want to hear. *You are lovely. You are kind. You are patient. You are exactly the sort of person who would send hardworking, low-earning philosophy authors $10.*

TL;DR: It's still unclear to what extent our personalities are formed by nature and nurture. Don't worry, there's always someone else to blame for your shortcomings (your parents, when in doubt).

The Archaeology of Foucault

How do we reconcile the idea of our personalities with the realisation of just how brittle they are? After all, we can alter them by eating a Mars bar, drinking a Long Island Iced Tea, or having a bad night's sleep. What if they're not fixed and presented to the world, as many people believe, but rather, created by it?

This was the thinking of French philosopher Michel Foucault. Archaeologists dig down into the ground to search for the bones and artefacts of our ancestors. Foucault felt we could take an archaeological approach to the history of thought. He was certain that if you'd been born a hundred years in the past, you'd be radically different—not because your personality would be dropped into a new time and forced to adapt, but because your personality is a social construct. It's built, in part, by the time and circumstances in which you live. In the same way, if humans could fly like birds, today we'd have a different society, with a wholly new understanding of what it is to be a human (and probably far less dodgy discount airlines).

An example Foucault elaborates on is the distinction between madness and sanity. If you were born five hundred years ago, you'd have no concept of mental illness. The town's loon probably wouldn't be considered mad but someone who merely possessed a very different kind of (difficult to monetise) wisdom. It's only around the time of the Enlightenment that the idea the mind could become ill and need help formed. Mental health is a social construct. Once created, it led to the very real construction of asylums (to house these newly diagnosed "mentally ill" people), which, in turn, led to a need for mental health professionals, such as psychologists, to work within them.

Rather than a fixed *you* looking out at the world, Foucault felt it was more accurate to say you are born as a *you*-shaped void that is gradually filled by the views and values of the society in which you live, filtered through the haze of your own experiences. It's from this lumpy, raw experience that we attempt to roll out a smoother fiction of ourselves and understanding of our personalities. Which explains why Foucault famously said: "I don't feel that it is necessary to know exactly what I am. The main interest in life and work is to become someone else that you were not in the beginning."

TL;DR: Foucault believed that human nature isn't a fixed constant but a condition defined by elements we are mostly unaware of. Consequently, a mid-level manager is not a caveman in better clothing, with less respect for mammoths, despite the effort of many managers to disprove this.

A Modern Man's Archaeology — An Authentic
Crime Scene

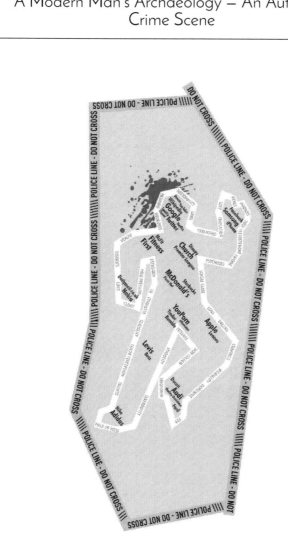

In the Cemetery of Dasein

If circumstances are so persuasive, and our personalities so intimately intertwined with them, how we can live authentically? How can we be our own people?

German philosopher Martin Heidegger felt he knew, calling his approach *Dasein* (*da* [German for "here"] and *sein* [German for "being"]). Traditionally, to explain something specific, philosophers start with the general and edge their way forward. They're particularly chuffed with themselves when by the time they've finished, their answers encompass everything, from the cosmos all the way down to the nuts and bolts of your personality. When trying to explain existence, they live by the motto "go big or go home".

Instead, Heidegger started the other way around, with personal experience, and worked upwards to more fundamental questions. This approach is called phenomenology: examining things through the experience of how they appear to us. Instead of asking "What is it to be a human?" ask, "What is it like?"

It's a unique trait of humans to bother themselves with what being is, he felt. Baked beans don't ask themselves why or what they are. They just are (delicious). Accordingly, he felt that it's only in comprehending this perspective of yourself, *the subjective you*, and your limitations in existence and time that you are allowed to live authentically. Dasein works like this.

1. A rock/tree/Mars bar is blissfully unaware of the concept

of existence; it just is in the world. Humans, on the other hand, not only exist but also *know* that they exist. As humans we can reflect upon our Dasein.

2. Because we know we are here, we are also conscious of the fact that one day we won't be, even if we decide to ignore this as much as possible. We're aware of our mortality. Death is what makes Dasein unique. No one else can experience our death. It's unique to us.

3. Thus, for Heidegger, death is not an end to a timely process but an authentic part of Dasein itself. It's only when we fail to recognise how much we are influenced by others, and our surroundings, that we become inauthentic. Reflecting more deeply on the mortality of existence elevates Dasein from being reactive to being authentic.

Of course, most of us would do anything to avoid being confronted by our own mortality. It's a flaw in our ~~Dasein~~ design. Heidegger challenged this in much of his work. For example, when asked how we could better lead our lives, he responded, "We should spend more time in cemeteries."

TL;DR: Martin Heidegger was a morbid German philosopher whose philosophy, Dasein, was a mix of YOLO and be true to yourself. He thought cemeteries should be more popular, somehow ignoring that people are already dying to get into them.

The Authenticity of Your Facebook Self

Sticking with the topic of authenticity, consider this: would philosophers say that our online personalities and friendships are authentic? Let's look at how the Internet, and in particular, Facebook, has changed relationships.

Pre-Internet friendships: *Depth not breadth.* A rather messy affair of back and forth that involved actually meeting other humans in real life and looking into their weird, lumpy faces. You had to know the person you wanted to call "friend", and perhaps have lent this person a drill. There was no need to prefix these friendships with the word "real".

Internet friendships: *Breadth not depth.* A mostly burdenless combination of likes, retweets, erratic emailing, and passive consumption of each other's status updates, mediated via communication templates provided by private companies: *"Sally is in a relationship with John", "Jim left his job at Burger King", "Robert likes that Steve likes that Robert is looking forward to the weekend".*

Perhaps rather than seeing modern friendship as having been plagiarised and diluted, it's better to accept that it's the latest development in what French philosopher Guy Debord called a spectacle. Debord argued (well before the Internet) that our fetish for possession led to the commoditisation of social life: "All that once was directly lived has become mere representation." Modern life is mostly a passive consumption of spectacles, all brought to us in flicker-free HD resolution by mass media. Private companies such as

Facebook commodify and depersonalise our interactions, optimising them for numbers not authenticity, or in Debord: "The decline of being into having, and having into merely appearing."

As shock, outrage, and celebrity clothing mishaps rip around the world one trending hashtag at a time, the spectacle gets grander, faster, and ever more fleeting. So it is with Internet friendships. They're friendships, just not as defined by us. They're "If Carlsberg made" friendships, "Just Do It" friendships, "I'm Lovin' It" friendships, sold back to us at a cost.

Debord was not media-phobic. He knew that to a certain extent, society needs these spectacles to exist. However, he wanted us to be aware of the trade-offs we make when we participate in society's spectacles. And what a show it is! Wanna be friends?

TL,DR: Facebook friends are not friends. They are part of a spectacle that makes a few people rich and most of the others anxious about how unphotogenic they are.

SEATING
30

Inauthentiphrenia

Inauthentiphrenia is a condition in which the sufferer is unable to live according to their own wishes and desires. Their ideals and actions are unduly influenced by the society around them. It is likely to manifest with the following symptoms:

Official Diagnosis

Symptoms

- Eating at a restaurant simply because it's busy
- Chinese calligraphy tattoos
- Liking The Beatles
- Possessing Tibetan prayer flags
- Owning scented candles
- Possession of Tibetan prayer flags
- Going on all-inclusive package holidays
- Owning practical, normcore clothing

Medication

After defecation, ingest 2 x 10mg Dasein and 20mg Eudaimonia.

For risks and side effects, please see the following information leaflet.

ORIGINAL

Dr. Willem u Tinkel
München, 29. März 2018

Medication

Dasein©

Medication
10mg Existence Enhancer.
5x Mortality Amplifier

Instructions
Take 2x Dasein tablets each day with one full
glass of your own limitations.

Known side-effects
Detachment from everyday consciousness.
Desire to spend time in cemeteries.
Cravings for baked beans.

MEMEMEME*MENINGITIS* — certainty of the
uniqueness of one's own existence and
death.

Eudaimonie©

Medication
20ml of pure reason, with additional
virtue+ supplement.

Instructions
Upon waking, rub virtue+ into a cleansed face,
to experience a full day of total self-control.

Known side-effects
Increased (fake) humility about one own's
knowledge.

Over-moderation in earthly things and a focus
on ideals.

In rare cases, it can lead to intensified usage
of antiquated words. *Blackguard.*

*If symptoms persist, please contact
a life coach immediately.*

ORIGINAL

TL;DR: Inauthentiphrenia is a (fictitious) illness suffered by inauthentic people and is best cured either with Heidegger's Dasein or Ancient Greece's eudaimonia.

CHAPTER 4

ATTITUDE AND PERSPECTIVE

Half
FULL

Half
EMPTY

50% AIR

50% WATER

Technically, the glass is always full.
The more important question is — what's in it?

Winning the Lottery, and Other Misfortunes

A young married couple walks arm in arm to a restaurant, where they're meeting friends for dinner. Out of nowhere, the heavens darken and a torrent of rain lashes down upon them. The couple spots a covered alleyway and takes shelter. "That was lucky," says the woman. "We could have gotten really soaked if we hadn't found this alleyway." "That was unlucky," replies her husband. "We're wet and now we'll be late to meet our friends."

Then the man spots a lottery ticket on the ground as the roof they're sheltering under is hit by lightning and collapses on top of them. "That was lucky," says the woman later, as they lie together in neighbouring hospital beds. "That lightning could have killed us." "That was unlucky," replies her husband. "We traded getting soaked on the street for broken bones."

Later, while flipping channels on the hospital TV, they find that week's lottery results. Remembering the ticket, the husband reaches painfully into his coat for it and discovers they've won the jackpot. "That was lucky!" says the woman. "We're rich!" "That was unlucky!" replies her husband. "Winning the lottery is always a curse."

Back home, in plaster, they receive a letter informing them that the lottery company's boss has absconded to Trinidad and Tobago with their winnings. "Oh well," says the woman, with a shrug. "Easy come, easy go. At least we still have each other, right?" "EASY COME, EASY GO?" her incredulous husband shouts, "A roof fell on my head! I broke several bones! Someone stole my lottery winnings. I'm married to someone who is always insufferably happy about everything! Sod you and your 'easy come, easy go'."

The couple gets divorced. "That was lucky," says the woman. "That miserable bastard is finally gone." "That was lucky," says the man. "That happy-go-lucky idiot is finally gone. When's the next flight to Trinidad and Tobago? I've got revenging to do."

Now, while this story is completely fictional, you'll probably find yourself empathising more with either the man or the woman's world view. In your opinion, who sees things more clearly? Is it better to frame your glass as half full, half empty, or merely one liquid receptacle in an open cocktail bar of limitless potential? How much control do you really have over your life, and if it's not much, should this bother you?

TL;DR: We all choose to perceive the things that happen to us in different ways. Cynics might say that marriage is to love what gigantism is to planet earth: a runaway solution searching for a problem. Fortunately, if it goes wrong, there's always revenge, therapy, and Trinidad and Tobago (for legal reasons, probably best done in that order).

The Stoics – They Couldn't Care Less

While we can't *not* have a perspective on the world, we can choose how to perceive it. This piece of practical wisdom is the cornerstone of a philosophical school of thought called stoicism. "The pain is not due to the thing itself, but to your own estimate of it," said Marcus Aurelius, stoic and one-time emperor of Rome.

The stoics felt sure that we don't just witness events. We also create stories about them, based on the way we want to see the world. Both the husband and wife in the previous seating lived the same experiences but told themselves completely different stories about them. While the wife preferred to view the events of her life as a happy Disney film, her husband preferred to view them as a Greek tragedy. Every time anything happens to you, you get to make that same choice and decide what stories to tell yourself. Every time someone treads on your foot or skips in front of you in the supermarket checkout line, you can view these acts as accidents, clumsiness, deliberate rudeness, or declarations of *!!ALL OUT WAR!!* In short, sticks and stones might break your bones, but perception will blow your head off.

According to famous stoics such as Epictetus and Marcus Aurelius, stoicism isn't about trying to stop telling yourself these stories, nor even about trying to change them to happier ones, but about merely acknowledging them. It's about trying to slowly untangle yourself from them, thus emotionally insulating yourself from the whimsy of your fate and the fallibility of your storytelling. It requires asking yourself what things are truly under your control. Only what you can directly change is relevant to your life, and these things are few. Everything else is simply not your concern.

Today, we often use the word "stoic" in sentences such as "you responded stoically to accidentally electrocuting yourself". It has almost become a synonym for being emotionless and indifferent. This is unfair to stoicism. It was never intended to be a macho stance of unemotional toughness, or a way to withdraw from life, but to be a practical way of living that involves not investing time and sorrow in what can't be changed. And the less time you spend interpreting life, the more time you'll have to enjoy living it.

TL;DR: Stoicism is a school of thought that tries to insulate us from the effect of the stories we tell ourselves about the things that happen to us. If you can't be a stoic, be a good storyteller. Spoiler alert: You're the hero. You live happily ever after.

Perspectivisms

There are several different perspectives we can take when shit happens. Here's a quick overview.

Hinduism: This shit has happened before.

Islam: If shit happens, it is the will of Allah.

Catholicism: If shit happens, you deserve it.

Fundamentalism: If shit happens, you will go to hell.

Judaism: Why does this shit always happen to us?

Creationism: God made all that shit.

Christian Science: When shit happens, don't call a doctor—pray!

Unitarianism: Come let us reason together about this shit.

Utopianism: This shit doesn't stink.

Darwinism: Let's see what this shit evolves into.

Capitalism: That's MY shit.

Communism: It's everybody's shit.

Feminism: Men are shit.

Chauvinism: We may be shit, but you can't live without "this" shit.

Commercialism: Let's package this shit.

Idolism: Let's bronze this shit.

Existentialism: Shit doesn't happen; shit IS.

Stoicism: This shit wasn't under your control anyway.

Hedonism: There's nothing like a good shit!

Jehovah's Witnesses: May we have a moment of your time to show you some of our shit?

Hare Krishna: Shit happens, rama rama.

Agnosticism: Shit might have happened; then again, maybe not.

Atheism: I don't believe this shit!

Nihilism: No shit.

Narcissism: I am the shit!

TL;DR: There are many perspectives you can adopt. Each one will change how you see your life, and quite possibly even how many lives you'll get.

Fact File: Marcus Aurelius

Influence: 6/10

Nationality: Roman

Dates: 26 April 121 AD – 17 March 180 AD

Groupies: Marcus' quotes are an essential part of every self-respecting motivational book, as well as an all-time favourite in-between slide for management PowerPoint presentations. George Washington, Wen Jiabao, and Bill Clinton all list *Meditations* as their favourite book.

· Aurel ·

Bio: Marcus Aurelius Antoninus Augustus was one of the most powerful philosophers to ever walk the earth, since his day job was being emperor of Rome. At the height of his power, he ruled almost the entire known world. Although he successfully waged wars, he's best remembered for his modesty and contemplative nature rooted in the philosophy of stoicism.

Greatest Idea: Marcus Aurelius is considered one of the five good emperors. None were as revered and loved as he, nor became as many statues. Though he's the poster child of stoicism and one of the most well-known philosophers of ancient times, he rarely wrote an original thought. He mostly collected and iterated the ruminations of his teachers and idols. We can forgive him, since he was also pretty busy fighting epic battles against the Parthians, Germans, and Britons for the glory of the Roman Empire (and posing for statues).

Worst Idea: Commodus. Marcus managed to father thirteen children during his thirty-year marriage. Since only five outlived him, it's understandable how attached he was to them. Back then, emperors normally selected one of their ablest generals or wisest senators for succession. Marcus broke with the tradition of his predecessors and inaugurated his wicked, cruel, dissolute son Commodus. Picking any random slave would have been more prudent. Just how bad was Commodus? Well, he's considered by history to be personally responsible for the rapid decline of the Roman Empire.

Anecdote: Imagine you've just come home from a successful military campaign. What would you do? Bathe in the public attention? Treat yourself to a confetti-filled parade? Not Marcus Aurelius. When he victoriously returned to Rome after a particularly gruelling war, he sold considerable parts of his personal possessions to help relieve the effects of famine and plague. After that, he cut taxes and founded schools, orphanages, and hospitals, and also helped pass legislation to improve the lives of slaves. He was almost offensively compassionate (either that, or he had some of the best PR people Ancient Rome could buy/enslave).

Quotes:

"Very little is needed to make a happy life; it is all within yourself, in your way of thinking." *But it often feels like not thinking (ignorance) is the better companion for bliss.*

"The art of living is more like wrestling than dancing." *That's not to say that the occasional wrestling move isn't also useful on the dance floor.*

"Everything we hear is an opinion, not a fact. Everything we see is a perspective, not the truth." *Everything that we hate thoroughly deserves our scorn, though.*

Marcus Aurelius in Objects:

1. Spanish poster: His family originated from the Spanish peninsula.

2. Weapons: Although it took him twenty years, he successfully fought off the fierce Germanic barbarians.

3. Stoa miniature: The so-called Stoa Poikile (i.e. "the painted porch"), from which his philosophy got its name.

4. Broken chains poster: His idol was Epictetus, a slave who later became a famous stoic philosopher.

5. First-aid kit (with gladiator blood): Gladiator blood was recommended by Roman physicians to aid various ailments, including infertility. After a gladiator was killed, vendors would often sell the still-warm blood to the crowd.

6. Pop-culture equivalent: Nelson Mandela. Also a national treasure, Mandela was beloved by his people but rose to power in difficult times then ruled with wisdom and restraint. He also makes for a great statute.

TL;DR: Marcus Aurelius was both a stoic and one of Rome's greatest emperors. It's with great foresight that he taught stoicism, since he gave no one a choice in regards to his heir, lumbering them with his brute son, Commodus, who almost single-handedly destroyed the empire his father created. If you aspire to lasting fame, or enjoy being defecated on by pigeons, erecting statues is a nifty idea.

The Walk of (Stoic) Fame

Here's an overview of stoicism in popular culture.

Spock: *Star Trek*'s pointy-eared pragmatist is perhaps the most famous fictional stoic. Spock, ever present and correct, is prone to saying really irritating things in times of crisis, such as, "What is necessary is never unwise" and "Pain is a thing of the mind. The mind can be controlled." Interestingly, the relationships he builds on the *Enterprise* regularly test the limits of his stoicism. In one episode, he's seen repeating the mantra "I'm in control of my emotions" before bursting into tears and momentarily losing said mind. An average Tuesday night for most of us.

Andy Dufresne: Remember how Red (played by Morgan Freeman) first described everyone's favourite wall mole in *The Shawshank Redemption*? "I could see why some of the boys took him for snobby . . . He strolled, like a man in a park without a care or a worry in the world, like he had on an invisible coat that would shield him from this place." Andy never gets angry with the system that falsely imprisoned him, for he can't change it. Instead, he gets busy chipping at the wall of his cell without knowing how thick it is, where it might lead him, and how draughty he's going to make his cell.

Sherlock Holmes: How did Arthur Conan Doyle's famous detective traverse Victorian London outthinking so many criminals? Elementary, my dear *Fast* Philosopher. He was a raging stoic who uttered things such as, "The emotional qualities are antagonistic to clear reasoning" and "Crime is common. Logic is rare." And we're pretty sure he then added, "Honest lawyers rarer still."

The Serenity Prayer: Alcoholics Anonymous (and similar organisations of twelve steppers) begin each session with a stoic prayer. You'll probably know its words but not its name: "God, grant me the serenity to accept the things I cannot change, the courage to change the things I can, and the wisdom to know the difference."

TL;DR: There have been many famous stoics in popular culture, such as Spock, Andy Dufresne, and Sherlock Holmes. Stoics don't usually start the party—they're more like the hyperrational, quiet irritant analysing it from the corner. They find it difficult to give up control since they know how little of it they had in the first place.

A Stoic's Guide to Picking Up Someone at a Party (Or Not Caring If You Can't)

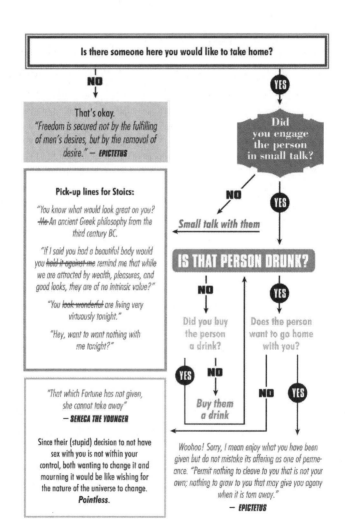

Is there someone here you would like to take home?

NO

That's okay.
"Freedom is secured not by the fulfilling of men's desires, but by the removal of desire." — **EPICTETUS**

Pick-up lines for Stoics:

"You know what would look great on you? ~~Me~~ An ancient Greek philosophy from the third century BC.

"If I said you had a beautiful body would you ~~hold it against me~~ remind me that while we are attracted by wealth, pleasures, and good looks, they are of no intrinsic value?"

"You ~~look wonderful~~ are living very virtuously tonight."

"Hey, want to want nothing with me tonight?"

"That which Fortune has not given, she cannot take away"
— **SENECA THE YOUNGER**

Since their (stupid) decision to not have sex with you is not within your control, both wanting to change it and mourning it would be like wishing for the nature of the universe to change.
Pointless.

YES

Did you engage the person in small talk?

NO → *Small talk with them*

YES

IS THAT PERSON DRUNK?

NO

Did you buy the person a drink?

YES / **NO**

NO → *Buy them a drink*

YES

Does the person want to go home with you?

NO / **YES**

Woohoo! Sorry, I mean enjoy what you have been given but do not mistake its offering as one of permeance. *"Permit nothing to cleave to you that is not your own; nothing to grow to you that may give you agony when it is torn away."*
— **EPICTETUS**

The Joys of Corruption and Why Morality Is for Losers

Some people feel that stoicism is cheating because it encourages you to step away from the world. These people would only ever agree to step away if it gave them more space to run screaming, fists raised, at the problems of existence. Society calls them crazy, and you can often find them in extreme-sport adverts.

But what if, maybe, they're onto something? Why not indulge fully in everything pleasurable, especially the physical? Isn't the longing to satisfy one's own desires just the logical conclusion of our mortality? And isn't discontent the biggest driver of change? Is morality not just a straight jacket for pleasure?

If you think so, you're probably a libertine. For libertines, "morality" is little more than the misguided attempt of others to limit their fun. Yet instead of calling others out for being spoilsports, the libertine is required to thank polite society for nudging them back onto the right, "virtuous" path. A path they're probably now planning to splash with Dom Pérignon and pink unicorn glitter.

Libertarians don't tend to be looked kindly upon by history, as proven by renowned hedonist Marquis de Sade. Sade was an aristocrat and sex addict who didn't believe in the state, private property, or having anyone infringe upon his liberties. Ironically, he spent more than thirty of his seventy-two years in private properties of the state (prisons and asylums), where he passed the time writing violent pornography. It's from his name that, today, we have the word "sadism".

Perhaps the only true test of morality and virtue is this: how would you live if you knew you could get away with anything? Italian philosopher Niccolò Machiavelli's *The Prince* deals with this exact question. He concluded that while peasants are free to worry about morality, leaders are busy stressing about legacy, their state, and sustaining power. For them, the ends justify the means. This idea proved so persuasive that, like de Sade, Machiavelli's legacy is his name: an adjective for any ruthless maverick.

Perhaps Machiavelli and Marquis de Sade fell onto history's wrong side merely because they didn't have the power to get away with their philosophies. This wasn't a problem for former US vice president Dick Cheney, when he went quail hunting and accidentally shot his friend in the face. Fortunately, his friend survived, and upon his release from hospital a week later, he said, "My family and I are deeply sorry for all that Vice President Cheney and his family have had to go through this past week." If you're powerful enough, people will even apologise to you for your shooting them in the face!

TL;DR: Is morality really a value in itself or just a function of your means to get away with stuff? Just in case, if you plan on shooting people in the face, be sure to obtain enough money/power to afford "rich white people's justice".

Getting the Female Perspective

You may have noticed that philosophy (and, accordingly, this book) is light on another important perspective—the female. For the past few thousand years, professional thinking has been somewhat of a testosterone fest. The men within that fest have either attempted to ignore contributions by women, or dismissed those women as "feminists" in the hope they would be ignored by everyone but other feminists. This should stop, and is stopping, but very slowly.

Here's an overview of the main ideas of nine of philosophy's female contingent:

Hypatia of Alexandria (365 – 415): Hypatia was the beloved leader of a Platonist philosophy school. She wrote mostly about the danger of religion and felt that humans lacked the mental capacity to comprehend complicated ideas, such as God. She was killed by an extremist group of Christians who cut her to death with oyster shells. "Reserve your right to think, for even to think wrongly is better than not to think at all," she said.

Mary Wollstonecraft (1759 – 1797): An English philosopher and one of its first feminists, she wrote "A Vindication of the Rights of Men." "Taught from infancy that beauty is woman's sceptre, the mind shapes itself to the body, and roaming round its gilt cage, only seeks to adorn its prison." At the age of only thirty-eight, she died from complications of childbirth, a birth that gave the world Mary Wollstonecraft Shelley, author of *Frankenstein.*

Ayn Rand (1905 – 1982): A divisive figure and poster woman for the American conservative and libertarian movements, Rand was a Russian-American novelist. Her defining philosophy was objectivism, which contains a pretty brutal idea of rational self-interest. She believed that since the individual and the individual's rights are sacred, people should act selfishly to further their goals. "The smallest minority on earth is the individual. Those who deny individual rights cannot claim to be defenders of minorities." She mostly saw government as a giant faff best avoided. "The question isn't who is going to let me; it's who is going to stop me."

Hannah Arendt (1906 – 1975): Arendt was a German-born Jewish philosopher who had to flee from the Nazi regime. Her works deal with the nature of political power, authority, and totalitarianism. She coined the phrase "the banality of evil" to describe how evil is not radical but rather a function of thoughtlessness: "The sad truth is that most evil is done by people who never make up their minds to be good or evil"; ". . . and the very magnitude of the crime the best excuse for doing nothing."

Simone de Beauvoir (1908 – 1986): Simone de Beauvoir was a French writer and philosopher considered the originator of the twentieth-century's feminist movement. Her most influential book is *The Second Sex*. In it she argues that women have been held back throughout history by the perception that they are divergent from the male norm. "Society, being codified by man, decrees that woman is inferior; she can do away with this inferiority only by destroying the male's superiority."

G. E. M. Anscombe (1919 – 2001): Gertrude Elizabeth Margaret Anscombe's most important work is her 1957 book *Intention*, which analyses the relationship between human action and various versions of will. It's often referred to as action theory (who said philosophers never get any action?). "Those who try to make room for sex as mere casual enjoyment pay the penalty: they become shallow. At any rate the talk that reflects and commends this attitude is always shallow. They dishonour their own bodies; holding cheap what is naturally connected with the origination of human life."

Philippa Foot (1920 – 2010): An English philosopher famed for her work in ethics (she penned the infamous trolley problem), Foot believed emotions are based on beliefs; therefore, if we can change our beliefs we can change our emotions. She was a prescient thinker on not just philosophy but also the folly of philosophers. "You ask a philosopher a question and after he or she has talked for a bit, you don't understand your question any more."

Judith Butler (1956 –): A contemporary American philosopher concerned with gender and sexuality, Butler believes that gender is performative (not fixed but rather a role we adopt). "We act as if that being of a man or that being of a woman is actually an internal reality or something that is simply true about us, a fact about us, but actually it's a phenomenon that is being produced all the time and reproduced all the time, so to say gender is performative is to say that nobody really is a gender from the start."

Anne Dufourmantelle (1964 – 2017): Dufourmantelle was a French philosopher, psychoanalyst, and risk-taker. "When there really is a danger that must be faced in order to survive . . . there is a strong incentive for action, dedication, and surpassing oneself." She argued against our security culture, which frowns on risk and so leaves a void in existence. She was probably not a fan of airports. She died tragically, while trying to save a friend's child from rough seas. "Being alive is a risk. Life is a metamorphosis and it begins with this risk."

TL;DR: Women could have had a huge influence on philosophy, but for most of the past two-and-a-half-thousand years, men either wouldn't let them or dismissed them simply as "feminists".

CHAPTER 5

HEDONISM AND CHOICE

The Supermarket of Life

Imagine that after your death, your soul arrives in a giant supermarket. You turn to the soul next to you, busy filling up its trolley with a package marked "Footballing Ability".

"Excuse me, what is this place?" you ask.

"It's the Supermarket of Life," the soul replies. "Pick out what you need for your next life. You can buy only one trolley's worth, and after you check out, that's it. You're reborn into your new life and won't remember this place."

You have many more questions, but the soul has already disappeared into the education aisle. You grab a trolley and begin exploring. The more luxurious the item, the larger it seems to be. Your trolley is small, so you pick sensibly. Old Age is the first thing you put in, along with Above Average Height, since you love basketball. Then you find space for a Modest Two-Room Apartment. You spend ages in the Life Partner section deciding between Partner 3000 and Partner 3200 Academic Edition.

Your trolley is already overloaded before you've finished with the basics: health; a modest home; a fitting partner; a degree. Unable to fit anything else in, you make your way to the checkouts dreaming about your new life. It's going to be great . . .

Lost in your thoughts, you crash into another soul, and from its overflowing trolley falls Partner 4000 Beauty Deluxe. It's like the 3000 but 25 percent more beautiful and with rich, old, generous parents. You are instantly jealous. "Excuse me, but where did you find Life Partner 4000?" you ask.

"Level 2. There's an elevator at the back. Got some great life upgrades there—PhD titles, exotic holidays, heated towel rails . . ."

You didn't know there was a level 2! You look down at your trolley. There's a good life in it, you're sure. But level 2 good? What else is up there? Amazing stuff, no doubt.

You go up. Just as promised, it's stocked full of amazing upgrades. You swap out your puny Master's for a PhD. Upgrade your partner to the 4000 Beauty Deluxe. You have to remove from the trolley a few tins of Humility Soup and PensionPlan+, and downgrade your thirty-five-hour workweek to sixty. But it'll be worth it, you figure.

Then, as you head towards the checkout again, there's an announcement over the loudspeaker. Level 3 is open. *Bastards.* You can only imagine what awesome upgrades there will be. Maybe there's Worldwide Fame™ or the rumoured Life Partner 5000 Millionaire Nymphomaniac Limited Edition. You look down at your trolley. Its contents no longer make you content.

You dance excitedly in the lift up to level 3. You step out of the elevator. The lights go out. The elevator disappears. "Welcome to level 3," a loud voice says. "You are visitor 75,987,072,335. This level exists only to prove that it's impossible for humans to ever be happy. You will now be reborn as a dung beetle. Thanks for visiting the Supermarket of Life."

TL;DR: Humans are never satisfied with what they have. The Supermarket of Life has only two levels. Smart people keep their feet on the ground. People who make mistakes in elevators are wrong on many levels.

Satisfaction's Short Shelf Life

The previous fable illuminates something you've probably experienced in your everyday life: satisfaction is short. Danny-Devito short. However happy you are, you can't help daydreaming about the next level. But if you reach that level, you only stare up lovingly at the next. It's a never-ending cycle of adaptation and expectation generally called the hedonic treadmill.

Of course, in our busy daily lives, it's really, really easy to forget this and to think that working extra hours to afford the bigger apartment with the balcony and its own parking space is going to make us happier in the long term than the small, dark one in which we currently dwell.

However, once we get that apartment, we'll simply get used to it, create a new base-level normal, and begin fantasising about the apartment opposite with the whirlpool. Philosophers all the way back in the fourth century already knew this. St Augustine wrote, "Desire hath no rest, is infinite in itself, endless, and as one calls it, a perpetual rack . . ."

But isn't having something to aspire to an essential part of the human experience? What gets us out of bed in the morning?

"To be without some of the things you want is an indispensable part of happiness," said Bertrand Russell. Perhaps the confusion comes from not understanding what we want. We don't actually want the new thing but the aspiration itself; in particular, the transition between what we already have and what we think we need/want to make us happy. In short, we're hooked on progress, not on possession. While a boring truism, it turns out it is the journey, not the destination.

Happiness isn't measured in absolute terms but remains relative as we adapt and desensitise. Or, as Robert Frost famously said, "Happiness makes up in height for what it lacks in length" (making it the opposite of marriage). Yet, in a famous study, researchers asked two radically different groups—lottery winners and victims of catastrophic accidents—about their happiness. Analysing the results, the researchers found that the accident victims reported to be as happy as the lottery winners just six months after their accident. The shelf life of happiness is short, and before long we revert to our default level.

The relativity of happiness is a good thing overall. Otherwise, there would be no chance for a street kid in Cambodia, a sheet-metal worker on the Ivory Coast, or a hundred year old in a care home in Belgium to be happy. The hedonistic treadmill is the great equaliser and we're all chained to it, stumbling and lurching our way towards happiness.

TL;DR: We define our wants in terms of specific things, such as "bigger house", "better job", or "neighbour's wife", but what we really want is the feeling of progress; the transition, not the possession.

Fact File: Epicurus

Influence: 4/10

Nationality: Greek

Dates: 341 BC – 270 BC

Bio: Epicurus was a Greek philosopher often characterised as a hedonist because he believed that the most important pursuit in life was that of pleasure. Yet his idea of hedonism, called ataraxia, is better interpreted as finding inner peace and contentment in simple things.

Greatest Idea: There's no need to fear gods. Epicurus lived in superstitious times and wondered, Why do bad things happen to good people? This question is so famous in philosophy that it's even got its own name: theodicy. He concluded that since it's obvious that evil exists in the world, either

1. the gods try to stop it but cannot; or 2. they can stop it but don't want to.

Either way, they are, in effect, impotent or detached. Hence, not worth worrying about. Quite a relief for all involved, except maybe God, but that no longer mattered to anyone.

Worst Idea: The common human is beyond help. Epicurus'

school, The Garden, was a lush commune for the senses. Yet he felt there was no point attempting to educate the common person outside its walls. He felt that the masses were incurably deluded and the powerful incurably corrupt. So, rather than interacting with the system, just join with your buddies and withdraw from it. If alive today, he'd probably be the sort of person who would tell you there's no point in voting. But not voting makes it much harder to feel self-righteous fury when the government seizes your Garden and converts it into luxury apartments.

Anecdote: While Epicurus is philosophy's poster child for hedonism, this is a crude caricature of his beliefs, which focused on cherishing the small pleasures and avoiding extremes. To slander him, people attributed legendary feasts of lavish excesses to him, saying that he vomited twice a day from overeating and took part in "notorious midnight philosophisings" with four women: Hedeia ("Sweety-Pie"), Erotion ("Lovie"), Nikidion ("Little Victory"), and Mammarion ("Big Tits"). If you find yourself invited to any "notorious midnight philosophisings" always bring protection (rationality, rhetorical fallacies, and condoms).

Quotes:

"Pleasure is our first and kindred good. It is the starting point of every choice and of every aversion..." *Isn't it funny how our childhood punishments (e.g. naps and spanking) become pleasures?*

"Death is meaningless to the living because they are living, and meaningless to the dead . . . because they are dead." *The situation changes dramatically should there be a zombie apocalypse, though.*

"Of all the things which wisdom provides to make us entirely happy, much the greatest is the possession of friendship." *Although possession of a big bag of rainbow Skittles runs pretty close.*

Epicurus in Objects:

1. Girl-power poster: He was all for equality and let women and slaves go where others would not.

2. Graffiti: This was written on the gate of The Garden.

3. A couch: Just like Freud, epicureans were keen on self-reflection and analysis and pioneered what we now call talk therapy.

4. Pop-culture equivalent: Jim Jones. Jones (of the Peoples Temple) was a charismatic hedonist who brought together a group of like-minded people (Jonestown was interracial, unheard of in 1955's Indiana, USA). He also believed that civilisation was somewhat of a lost cause. He just approached it in a much more extreme, psychotic, jungles-of-Guyana, fizzy-drink, mass-suicide kind of way.

TL;DR: Epicurus was the hedonistic leader of his own mini school/cult called The Garden. Often portrayed as philosophy's greatest hedonist, he really espoused ataraxia, i.e. finding inner peace and contentment in simple things. Which makes you wonder why we made "simpleton" an insult. And a president.

Philosophy Happiness Kits — More Bliss Than You Can Contemplate

1. Breasts and chocolate bar: "Pleasure and action make the hours seem short." - *William Shakespeare*

2. Pain medication: "All happiness is an illusion. Life oscillates like a pendulum, back and forth between the pain and boredom." - *Arthur Schopenhauer*

3. Chain, handcuffs and whip: "It is always by way of pain one arrives at pleasure." - *Marquis de Sade*

4. Sad emoticon: "There is no record in human history of a happy philosopher." - *H.L. Mencken*

5. Mirror: "Happiness depends upon ourselves." – *Aristotle*

6. Moustache: "No intelligent man wears a moustache voluntarily – you can write that down" – *Sam Neil*

7. Light bulb: "Happiness is the feeling that power increases—that resistance is being overcome." - *Friedrich Nietzsche*

8. Tie and Family on Board sticker: "The serious happiness of most men depends upon two things: their work and their human relations." - *Bertrand Russell*

9. Coffee cup and cupcake: "Never underestimate the importance of being properly caffeinated and you can never be unhappy if you're holding a cupcake." - *Common Sense*

10. Duff Beer: "To alcohol! The cause of, and solution to, all of life's problems" - *Homer Simpson*

The Tyranny of Choice

Imagine two supermarkets: the first is in a former Eastern Bloc country before the fall of the Iron Curtain, and the second is a Walmart. Now, picture yourself in need of cereal. Which would you rather go to? Obviously the one with more selection, right?

Our happiness is defined by the choices we make. So, is it fair to say that the more options we have to choose from, the happier we will be? You probably want shout emphatically: "YES OF COURSE WHAT KIND OF QUESTION IS THAT?"

Yet for many philosophers, choice is not such a clear-cut, benign thing. Many choices contain hidden costs. Consider the French philosopher Jean-Paul Sartre. He argued that all people are born free, and that this is an irrevocable fact of our existence. So far so good. *Freedom!* But in Sartre's view, our individual freedom is not a gift to be revered but rather an existential curse. We are fundamentally free, which means that we are the only one responsible for our actions. In this sense, total freedom is total responsibility. Herein lies the problem, for we can never possibly know all the consequences of the choices we're forced to make. It's like having to pack your luggage without knowing where the plane will drop you off. No matter how much you love your favourite Hawaiian shirt, it will be of little use to you when you're shivering in the middle of a penguin colony at the South Pole.

Many studies show that once we have a few choices, adding more just makes us less able to decide, and less happy with what we decide. Yet not making a decision is rarely an option, unless you're a politician. Thus, we must simply live with the consequences of what we choose, no matter the lack of foresight or flawed reasoning that led us to that decision in the first place.

By making decisions, we inadvertently kill off infinite (often better) options. And once you start debating hypothetical trade-offs in your head, you're bound to lose, as the grass is always greener on the (imaginary) other side. Which leaves you on this side, in the weeds, left to be defendant, prosecutor, judge, jury, and executioner of all the decisions you've made, and without the means to foretell the verdict.

And so, we find ourselves hunched over, straining under the weight and burden of choice, trying to make peace with what we've picked while mourning all that we didn't: all the alternate lives we're not living; brownies we're not eating; people we're not dating; holiday destinations we haven't visited but which friends are posting about on our social media timelines. That leaves us with our final and perhaps hardest choice: how much do we let ourselves suffer for what we have and haven't chosen?

TL;DR: Choice is certainly better than no choice. But too much choice is a bit like too much sugar—it makes you behave weirdly and will ultimately lead to unhappiness (and diabetes).

Free Will and Other Fictions

The debate about choice leads us nicely to one of the most cherished concepts of human existence: ~~denial~~ free will. Because what sense does it make to have choices if you're never actually free to choose? How many of your choices are truly your own? A lot, you probably think. Well, imagine you're on a work trip and during lunch, you're offered two choices: a healthy salad or a plate of deliciously greasy fries. Which do you pick?

The competition was probably over once you smelled the fries, wasn't it? Well, not if you believe in free will. Then you must also believe that you were the sole arbiter of that decision and that while you're digging into a plate of tasty fries you could just as easily be chewing on some boring green rabbit food.

Let's elaborate on your decision a little bit more. Not in terms of blood pressure or cholesterol but in terms of what, ultimately, led you to make it. Is it possible that factors outside of your control influenced you to pick the fries? For example, your genes? Your nutrition education? Fond memories of home-made, deep-fried deliciousness? Your dad always made such good fries. Or was time to blame? You were in a rush. Maybe, in the end, it's a mix of all these things that swayed you to the fries? But then what happened to free will? See, it's complicated. Philosophy gives you two stands upon which to hang your hat.

1. Causality and determinism – "I did it because I was always going to do it."

Every action is connected to the circumstances that "caused" it. Free will dissolves into a lineage of linked causes and effects. "Making a decision" is really just the time it takes for the already made decision to be communicated to you. Your decisions are decided solely by causality.

2. Indeterminism – "I did it because it is the thing I did."

You have free will. That's the good news; your decisions are not predetermined. But this raises a question: if the decisions are not causally connected to you and all that defines you (i.e. your memories, genes, education, upbringing, etc.), how can they be called *your* decisions? Free will becomes non-existent, impersonal, and random. Like getting accidentally slapped in the face by a blind ghost.

Most philosophers have settled on the idea that free will is a helpful illusion, similar to how Photoshopped images help to sell makeup but aren't necessarily accurate portrayals of reality. They see the world as broadly deterministic but too complex to be predicted, and that *feels* like free will, or, as John Galsworthy said, "Life calls the tune, we dance." Perhaps the best quote to summarise this human condition is Schopenhauer's: "A man can surely do what he wills to do but cannot determine what he wills."

TL;DR: Causality and free will are two concepts that don't work well together. Unfortunately, neither one of them helps make salad taste better.

SEATING
43

Don't Be Sorry about Regret

Knowing that we have to make decisions, and can't know their consequences, leads to another interesting question: why do we regret? When was the last time you woke up and said to yourself, "Today is the day I'm going to make a deliberately wrong decision"?

If every decision is the logical conclusion of the situation in which it was made, how is regret even possible? All of its variables have expired. You can't go back in time, and even if you could, you wouldn't know the outcome of changing the supposedly regret-worthy decision anyway. Perhaps it would lead to more regret, or World War III. It's the classic time-traveller's dilemma. Today, you might regret having not punched your high school bully when you were sixteen, but you've no idea if having done so would have made him leave you alone or throw you off a bridge. Perhaps suffering under this bully is what's made you the kind, empathetic human being you are today.

If you don't regret who you are, how can you regret what made you who you are? Especially if you have no idea what made you who you are? Just as with free will, the more you try to get a firm grip on regret, the harder it thrashes to get away.

It's more likely that while we think we're regretting a specific decision, what we're actually feeling sorry about is a complicated mixture of the following:

- Not having known that piece of crucial information that would have made us make a different decision
- The fact that the great qualities we learnt from the bad decision couldn't have been learnt without it having occurred.
- Never getting to know how things would have played out had we chosen differently

Perhaps Danish philosopher Søren Kierkegaard was right when he said, "Marry, and you will regret it; don't marry, you will also regret it . . . Laugh at the world's foolishness, you will regret it; weep over it, you will regret that too . . . Hang yourself, you will regret it; do not hang yourself, and you will regret that too . . . This, gentlemen, is the essence of all philosophy." Regret, while useless when focused on a specific decision, becomes useful when it causes us to reconsider the maxims, doctrines, and thought processes that resulted in our making the fateful decision in the first place.

TL;DR: Regret is mostly pointless and illogical but a useful tool for philosophical inquiry and the basis of enormous amounts of poetry, music, and tacky apology cards.

Don't Buy Into Atonement

Regardless of whether we should regret our sins, can we atone for them? In the Middle Ages you certainly could. The Catholic Church pioneered these things called indulgence vouchers. Not only could sinners repent, they could also get rid of their sins altogether and avoid the hot flames of Purgatory simply by splashing a little cash. In essence, this deal was the lustful dream of any true businessman; the Church sold a product everyone needed (and it had a notoriously broad definition of "sin") and that had almost no production costs, a high profit margin, no competition, and couldn't be tested until the customer died, at which point it was too late for him or her to ask for a refund.

The going was good for a while. Sadly for the Church, public opinion, with the help of a certain Martin Luther, did eventually decide that if it looks like a duck and sounds like a duck, it's probably an elaborate, money-making, atonement-voucher scam. It was gotten rid of. *Or was it?*

You may have noticed that many products in our everyday-happy-consumer world are sprinkled with ethical upgrades that promise us peace of mind. Atonement for an unequal world in which consumerism results in the impoverishment of farmers, child labour, and the overuse of the world's natural resources. For instance, buying a cup of coffee used to be a straightforward transaction: coffee, money, acidity stomach-ache. Now, when buying a coffee, you're bombarded with options that promise to offset any guilt you might feel for the consumption: "fair trade," recyclable cups, tip jars, charity boxes. Indulgence vouchers made modern. Create the guilt. Sell the salvation. Only now, your redemption happens in this life, not the afterlife. "Capitalism with a human face," as philosopher Slavoj Žižek calls it.

It's also safe to assume that Big Coffee Corp., like any other global company, won't spend their shareholders' money unless it helps them to earn more of it. "Fair-trade" beans might cost you a dollar more, but it's likely that only a small percent of that makes it into the pocket of the poor Peruvian farmer. The main benefactor is still probably Big Coffee Corp. In "helping" people to feel better about buying its products, it thereby sells more, at a higher markup.

Maybe as Oscar Wilde suggested, the worst slave owners were the nice ones, for they helped to prolong a corrupt system that should have been forced to collapse. How complicit are we in prolonging the broken system that created the need for fair-trade products in the first place? Should we stop sustaining the Peruvian farmer in his misery and delaying him from finding a better use for his labour, such as becoming a football agent?

In the end, atonement upgrades are probably neither cynical profit-raising initiatives nor benign altruism. They're something in the middle. Atonement offers the chance not just to buy something, but also to buy into something. The morality of it is flexible and really just an obfuscation. In the end, the most important thing is to be conscious of the value system you're buying into.

TL;DR: Atonement is never truly possible. Morality is like mortality. It's abstract, complex, and important, but thinking about it too much just ruins everything. After bottled water, cryptocurrencies, and free hugs, indulgence vouchers are the ultimate business model.

Modern-Day Atonement

INDULGENCE VOUCHERS $1 each

These Vouchers entitles the bearer to atonement for the sin of:

VOUCHER
REPLYING TO A LONG PERSONAL EMAIL WITH JUST ONE SENTENCE E.G. "SOUNDS GOOD!"

VOUCHER
FEEDING A TROLL

VOUCHER
LIKING YOUR OWN STATUS UPDATE

VOUCHER
BLAMING YOUR FART ON THE DOG

VOUCHER
PRETENDING YOU DON'T LIKE A SONG JUST BECAUSE IT'S POPULAR

VOU...
LYING TO YOUR FRIEND ABOUT THE BEAUTY OF THEIR NEWBORN BABY

SOCIETY AND FAIRNESS

Hello, Human Number 7,000,500,001
aka Sarah Smith

Welcome to society! People are nice (mostly).
Chocolate is divine. Snow is cold. Kittens are
adorable etc. etc. You're going to love it,
probably. Anyway, we've signed you up.

The rules:
1) Land, property, and resources are private and
   don't belong to you unless they previously
   belonged to your parents.
2) Respect all our laws, or we'll put you in jail.
3) Don't tell anyone about Fight Club.

All very fair. Probably. Enjoy your existence
(optional, but will make you more popular at
parties).

Love,
THE GOVERNMENT.

PS: We also started some wars and used up some
resources. You owe us a few billion $s.
Hope that's okay xxx

Everyone Is Biased Against Me, Including Me

Pretend a politician has proposed a fantastic new national holiday—a day so brilliant, so relaxing, so inspiring that it will become the nation's favourite day. All year long people will look forward to it and count down to it on their calendars. A day where different generations will sit in harmony sharing stories, improving friendships, feeling loved, and appreciating all that they have in their lives. Adults, drunk and happy, will conceive more children on this day than on any other.

Sound good? Just to be extra fair, the government decides to hold a public referendum on whether to introduce it.

Would you vote for or against this new national holiday?

Now what if I told you that for this day to be introduced there must be 45 million murders? Hundreds of millions of people will experience the happiest day of the year, a day of unity, a day for family, but to compensate for that, there must also be 45 million murders on this special day, every year.

Now how would you vote?

Now what if I told you it's not humans who are murdered but turkeys? Every year on this public holiday, called Thanksgiving, 45 million turkeys will be killed.

Would you change your vote? Animals die every day for our food, so what's the difference?

Now what if I also told you that to enjoy Thanksgiving and to understand the turkey's sacrifice, you have to kill one turkey yourself?

Want to change that vote?

Okay, here's the last piece of information that I have for you. What if I were to inform you, with 100 percent certainty, that you'll be reincarnated as a turkey?

For the last time, would that change your vote?

 **YES** **NO**

TL;DR: How we vote depends very much on whether we're affected by the outcome, not on absolute morality. It's not a good idea to be a turkey on Thanksgiving, or possibly any time at all. Gobble, gobble.

The Original Position (SFW)

Most people would say that when it comes to politics, they vote in a fair and balanced way. They analyse the candidates, listen to their proposals, and vote for whoever they think will bring the most benefit to society. As we tried to show in the last seating, even if we think we're being fair and balanced, it's likely we'll vote for whatever brings us the most benefit and just rationalise the morality of it afterwards. The turkey and the human eating the turkey are going to vote very differently about Thanksgiving.

In Ancient Rome, people living on the periphery of the empire weren't permitted to vote on whether nearby lands should be invaded. The reasoning was that retaliation attacks from nearby settlements were most likely to occur on settlements at the edge of the Roman Empire. Makes intuitive sense, right? However, following the same chain of logic, could it not also be argued that the people who lived in the centre of Rome were equally biased about their (relative) safety? Soldiers must fight, so they are certainly biased. Their wives risk losing their husbands, which makes them equally conflicted (perhaps in both directions). Keep going and you quickly run out of voters, especially when we consider that even if the outcome is of no interest to us, we're still biased by our experiences, upbringing, morality, and irrationality when giving our two cents.

John Rawls is one of the philosophers who looked at the problem of how decisions could be made fairly. He called his solution the original position. It works like this:

1. For a vote to be fair, like the vote for Thanksgiving, all the people taking part need to be behind a "veil of ignorance".
2. This means that they can't know anything about themselves that would bias them—not their age, their race, their gender, their strengths, their intelligence, their handicaps, their talents, their values, society's values, nor their standing

within society. They can't know if they're one of the happy, feasting humans or one of the turkeys to be feasted upon.

3. Behind this veil of ignorance, they can vote freely for the benefit of everyone, judging each proposal on its actual merits. Only then, after the vote, is it revealed to the voters who they are, turkey or human, and, therefore, whether how they voted has helped or hindered them (if the latter, they'd probably shout FOWL-play).

Obviously, the original position is purely hypothetical, since we're born into a biased, existing society already in motion. We can't just start again. The veil is off. So how can we best structure society, then? One hugely influential philosopher, Confucius, thought he knew.

TL;DR: John Rawls argued that we can only vote without bias only in the original position—a position in which we know nothing about ourselves (not our age, gender, class, status, etc.). If Rawls had his way, turkeys might actually vote for Thanksgiving.

Fact File: Confucius

Influence: Europe 2/10; Asia 10/10

Nationality: Chinese

Dates: 551 BC – 479 BC

Groupies: Two thousand years of Chinese society

·K'ung-tzǔ·

Bio: Confucius lived during the Warring States period, a time of great turbulence. Dismayed by the chaos he witnessed, he sought constants in a world of change, hoping that order and unity could be restored if people respected traditions.

Greatest Idea: The five relationships. At the centre of his teachings are the five relationships that govern our lives, from top to bottom:

1. Sovereign to subject
2. Father to son
3. Husband to wife
4. Elder sibling to younger sibling
5. Friend to friend

According to Confucius, a good relationship is characterised by loyalty and adhering to the rituals, duties, and behaviours expected in each relationship. Society is improved not by abstract ideals but in leading by example. By respecting our position in life, and respecting its rituals, we form a more just society.

Worst Idea: Trickle-down morality. Confucius was convinced that society had to be changed from the top down. A just ruler who respected traditions would be the shining example that compelled all others to follow in his footsteps. Perhaps this is why he became a judge, which didn't work out all that well, since he was later mobbed out of office. Also, his own ideas didn't spread top down as he imagined, but only succeeded once they were applied bottom up via a grassroots movement of his disciples.

Anecdote: Confucius believed in meritocracy, and admitted students to his school regardless of class and social standing. The practice remained, and soon anyone who wanted to obtain an official position in the Chinese empire had to prove his aptness by passing written examinations. This might be one of the key reasons Chinese culture has been culturally and technologically ahead of the West for much of the last two millennia. Nevertheless, Confucius died thinking he was an utter failure, unaware that his teachings would come to define Chinese culture.

Quotes:

"It does not matter how slowly you go as long as you do not stop." *Not what she said.*

"To know what you know and what you do not know, that is true knowledge." *But probably far less profitable than selling your ignorance.*

"Choose a job you love, and you will never have to work a day in your life." *Alternatively, never work a day in your life and you'll automatically never have to choose a job! Yay!*

Confucius in Objects:

1. Walking stick: He roamed the feudal lands of China to find support for his teachings.

2. Judge's gavel: He became a judge at the age of fifty.

3. Bruce Lee poster: The name Confucius is the Latinized version of K'ung Fu-tzu (Great Master K'ung), the name given to him by his disciples.

4. Family tree: Confucius' family tree is the longest recorded in the world, now in its eighty-third generation.

5. Respect Your Elders sticker: This idea was the cornerstone of his philosophy, as he believed virtue springs from adhering to tradition.

6. Men Only sticker: He believed people need education to learn right from wrong, yet he thought women should be excluded from the educational system.

7. Pop-culture equivalent: Principal Skinner from *The Simpsons*. Both are educators struggling to win respect for their methods. Principal Skinner is forever trapped between what he wants (freedom, a relationship with Edna Krabappel) and his strict sense of duty to his mother, no matter how badly she treats him. Both are idealists who want to better society through education, and neither have much success (in their lifetimes).

TL;DR: Confucius wanted you to know your place, stay in it, and respect your elders to better all society. He believed society is improved not by abstract ideals but in leading by example. Maybe he was right; maybe he was just *confusedcius*.

East vs West Philosophy (Very Simplistically

	Western Philosophy	Eastern Philosophy
What were their greatest hits?	The rational and scientific schools, Christianity	Buddhism, Confucianism, Taoism, Zen, Yoga
And the fundamental difference?	We dissect.	They collect.
What does that mean?	Well, if the sciences are a puzzle, we are perfectly happy just taking a piece at a time and obsessing over it until only professional puzzlers know what's going on.	They want to solve everything—all the pieces have to fit together in a nice, neat, holistic, completed puzzle of life.
Can you tell me that again, but in Philosopher?	We focus on singular events and the role of the individual. Truth is found in the external world through research and the analysis of precise natural laws uncovered through logic and deduction. Focus is on specific problems via fragmentation of the disciplines. The truth must be both found and proven.	They take a more cosmological and systematic approach, seeing all events in the universe as interconnected. The truth is given, not found in experiments. It's revealed via introspection and the search inside yourself (often in the form of meditation). General knowledge and overarching context are essential.
Beliefs and values?	Outside in.	Inside out.
Once again, in Philosopher?	Success and achievement are mostly measured by external factors (money, faith, popularity, etc.) The individualistic nature of a person's personality is revered and encouraged. You should be critical and question the status quo.	Your inner world and your ability to control it are of the highest value. The way to the top is inside yourself, through self-development. Individualism is not virtuous.
Tell me about myself.	You and your soul are stable and fixed. There's a division between body and mind.	You need to find your true self. The only division is in your mind.
Role of religion in philosophy?	Enemies.	Best buddies.

TL;DR: Western philosophy is outside in; the answers are there to be discovered. Eastern philosophy is inside out; the answers are inside of us. If you do go looking for answers inside of yourself, consider using intellectual lubricant.

Why Organs Like Opt-Out Contracts

It's estimated that every day, three people in Germany die while waiting for an organ transplant. Not that there aren't enough organs —just not enough donors. While around 70 percent of German citizens *say* they'd be happy to donate their organs, only about 12 percent of people make that possible. Organ donation in most of the world is an opt-in system, and it requires a donor identification card.

Many of us never get around to opting in for the simple reason that, despite our good intentions, we're busy, forgetful, and don't relish being confronted with something as inconvenient as our own mortality. Plus, there are just so many delicious new cakes to try and TV shows to binge on. The government invests millions in raising awareness about the importance of organ donation to try to encourage us, but those efforts haven't been very successful.

But there are other approaches to this problem. For instance, Austria has managed to convince a staggering 99.98 percent of their citizens to be organ donors! What miracle technique have they used to educate their citizens? Simple: they made organ donation part of an opt-out system instead of an opt-in one. If you're an Austrian citizen, unless you explicitly opt out (a simple letter will suffice), your organs belong to other Austrians and will be claimed at your death. Why do just 0.02 percent of people opt out? For a similar reason so few of us explicitly opt in—a mix of apathy, laziness, and ignorance (they simply don't know they need to). And maybe, also, they have a desire to help others.

All societies subject their citizens to a mixture of opt-in and opt-out contracts. Voting, charity, volunteering: all opt-in. Your job, home, clubs, societies, marketing calls to your phone, spam e-mail: all opt-out. But when exactly did you opt in to the very society that contains all these various contracts? And how does it work?

Well, it requires a special contract of its own. Like the Austrians and their innards, few know that they've opted in to it. And it's impossible to opt out of this one. It's called the social contract.

TL;DR: Society works on a mixture of opt-in and opt-out contracts. The über contract, which you opt in to at birth and can't opt out of, is called the social contract. Think of it as a cable TV service contract for all of society. Only it's more flexible, since you can get out of it by dying.

The Fine Print of Society

Until the eighteenth century, power was distributed in a straightfor-ward manner, with just two clear models:

1. **Natural order:** This model is just like Aristotle's ladder; there are stones at the bottom and monarchs, inbred dukes, and royalty on top. How "natural" this seemed likely depended on how high up someone was in this order. Conveniently, the higher-ups also had the power to enforce its heirachy on those below them.

2. **Divine law:** In this model, the right order of things is revealed by God to disciples. Coincidentally, the adherents of divine order often got a lucky break, with God decreeing they should be on the very top of it! The argument for adhering to a divine law, instead of a human-made law, was that since gods never err, how could they have gone amiss in choosing a particular clergyman, cast of priests, circle of shamans, or Prince Phillip?

Whether the order was natural or divine didn't matter much to anyone not on its summit. For rocks, plants, peasants, and serfs, both systems were deeply Machiavellian (dog eat dog), no matter who exactly got to be top dog.

Neither of these models satisfied French philosopher Jean-Jacques Rousseau. He believed that we were born free into a world he referred to as "the state of nature", a state without taxes and governments and all the other discontents of society. Yet all around him he found only evidence that "man is born free, but everywhere he is in chains".

Rousseau was not naive. He knew we couldn't all live in the woods autonomously without society and its awesome electric toothbrushes, multiscreen cinemas, and caramel waffles. The state of nature would be no picnic. Philosopher Thomas Hobbes said that our lives there would be "solitary, poor, nasty, brutish and short".

Nevertheless, Rousseau concluded that if we must be "enslaved", we might as well do it of our own free choosing, based on agreed rules of mutual enslavement. That way we give up some rights but get in return some protections, and so regain our autonomy. While I lose the right to murder you, you also lose the right to murder me (without consequences or high legal bills). It sounds like a simple idea, but it changed the legitimisation of ruling forever. We now had another option: a social contract.

The people would become the sole sovereign and legitimate true power. They would give up some rights for some protections. Suddenly we had a framework that allowed for inalienable rights, private property, the vote, representation—all based on an ever-developing set of laws. Today, the social contract is at the heart of almost every constitution. The catch? It's an opt-in contract, signed on our behalf at birth. There's no out, beyond death.

TL;DR: Nobody is an island. True autonomous freedom doesn't work if you want to have to a society. However, we don't have to be enslaved by natural order or divine law. Instead, we can choose to mutually forfeit some of our rights to each other via a social contract. Slavery is best done as a DIY project.

A Crass Look at the Cracies

-cracy (from the Greek *-kratia*: "power, rule"): a suffix denoting a form of rule or government.

Corporatocracy: Government by corporations or government entities with some private components. "You want what, citizen? A weekend? Hmm. Let me check with the nice people of Big Oil and Big Tobacco and get back to you."

Demarchy: Government by random selection (e.g. lottery). "You, sir, man at the back in the hat. Congratulations, you're now chancellor. *All hail the chancellor!*"

Fascism: Government by a totalitarian government or individual who cannot be democratically removed from power. "I rule because shut up or I will kill you."

Kakistocracy: Government by the least-qualified/least-principled citizens. "We rule because we've never ruled before and I mean, why not? How hard can it be? You over there, build me a marble palace shaped like my face."

Meritocracy: Government by people who have best demonstrated their talents, ability, or merits. "Watch me juggle these pot plants. I'm clearly the right person to become Juggle Minister of the Interior."

Monarchy/Aristocracy: Government by a few elite individuals or just one, in the form of a king or queen. "I rule because I'm the son of the last person who ruled. My credentials? I've just told you my credentials."

Oligarchy: Government by a small elite group of society (usually royal, wealthy, military, intellectual, or religious). "A vote for us is a vote for, well, to be honest, I'm pretty sure we're going to win. So, vote how you like."

Panarchracy: A hypothetical political philosophy that gives individuals the right to change their government/jurisdiction without having to move. "IRS? Stop writing me letters. Yes, I live in Atlanta, but I've decided to be governed by the Micronesian island of Nauru. Tax? Ha. Nauru has 0 percent income tax."

Plutocracy: Government by the richest. "We rule because our bank account says we rule. Here, have fifty dollars and go away."

Technocracy: Government by engineers, scientists, and other assorted nerds. "I *like* life much better since we voted Facebook into the Ministry of Communications."

Theocracy: Government by a god but administered by a church or religious group in God's name. "God told me I should be ruler. He told you that as well? Well, he told me to tell you that he was mistaken. Guards, in God's name, seize this man, and, also, make me a sandwich."

TL;DR: There are many different models of government, including kakistocracy (rule by the least qualified) and theocracy ("God told me I rule"). The only constant is that it's always more fun on top.

Ethics: The Really, Really Short Version

A social contract is all well and good. But what about personal contracts? How should we treat each other? What should we consider fair? Probably the most famous personal contract is the maxim of reciprocity found in nearly all ethical teachings: "Do unto others what you would have them do unto you." It's called the golden rule, and it mustn't be confused with the gold rule: "Whoever has the gold makes the rules."

Most of us can agree it's a pretty good way to live. Be nice to others because you want them to be nice to you. It's a simplistic ethical code of reciprocity, and that's probably why it has endured for thousands of years.

However, in the wrong hands, the golden rule has its dangers. There are quite some differences in what people "like" to have done to them. If you can't think of an example, fire up Google and type in any two words you thought couldn't possibly serve as a fetish and be proven instantly wrong. One person's fun foreplay is another person's lifetime of therapy. Blindly following the golden rule might lead you to some dark places, figuratively and literally.

Not convinced? Consider the following scenario. There's a knock at the door, and when you answer it, you find a man holding an axe that's covered in blood. He's calm—far calmer than you'd expect a man holding an axe covered in blood to be. He says he's looking for a friend of yours. "Do you know where she is?" he asks. You know where she is.

What should you do?

Lying violates the golden rule, unless you want to be part of a society of liars. However, following the golden rule here, you run the risk of sentencing your friend to a violent and premature death.

Because of these loopholes, many philosophers have criticised the golden rule, the most prominent being Immanuel Kant. He believed the external rules of how to behave, those given to us by other people, will always fall short. Internal rules we give ourselves sound better in principle, but then how can we be sure that we all have the same ethics? He wanted ethics to be both an absolute, irrefutable universal law, and self-imposed. Right had to stay right, no matter the day of the week or whether you liked it or not.

Kant felt, therefore, that we should trust in rationality. Just as 1 + 1 = 2 no matter who calculates it, rationality could provide the same set of ethical rules for any rational being. He developed the golden rule further: act as if all your actions would become a universal rule for everyone else. Or, expressed in Kantian (like Klingon but less comprehensible), "Act only in accordance with that maxim through which you can at the same time will that it become a universal law."

So now, instead of making your own preferences the arbiter of rules, you must come up with rules that fit all rational agents. This is the categorical imperative, and if you live it, in Kant's eyes, you live morally. In our hypothetical scenario, telling the man with the axe the truth is required because moral actions do not derive their worth from their expected consequences. If you lie to the man you are a means to an end, and deny the rationality of another person, which undermines there being free rational action at all.

TL;DR: Kant tried to formulate a universal moral law, which he called the categorical imperative. This sounds good, until you know that Kant would not have lied to an axe murderer who asked for your whereabouts. The categorical imperative is not to be confused with the *cat*egorical imperative: cats must always do whatever the hell they want.

SEATING
54

Platinum Rules

If you ever wondered why Moses came back from Sinai with only ten rules, when so much of life could profit from a little regulation and restriction, imagine having to schlep stone tablets all the way down a mountain.

If you're not a big fan of the categorical imperative, the golden rule, or modern systems of fun restriction like the Ten Commandments, here are a few other life rules you could adopt.

I

Don't argue with an idiot.
They only bring you down to their
level then beat you with experience.

II

Always be yourself,
unless you can be a unicorn.
In which case be a unicorn.

III

The secret to any happy relationship
is low expectations.

IV

If you need to ask the price,
you can't afford it.

V

Ask for forgiveness, not permission.

VI

Some days you're the pigeon;
some days you're the statue.

VII

Everybody is somebody else's
weirdo.

VIII

Experience is a wonderful thing.
It enables you to recognize a
mistake when you make it again.

IX

You can go anywhere you want if
you look serious, wear a white
coat, and carry a clipboard.

X

A balanced diet is a muffin
in each hand.

XI

If at first you don't succeed,
skydiving is not for you.

XII

People who want to share their
religious views with you never
want you to share yours with them.

XIII

A conscience is what hurts when all
of your other parts feel good.

CHAPTER 7

REALITY AND CONSCIOUSNESS

REALITY:

Worst game ever

Matrix²

You've never felt truly comfortable in this life. Sure, it has its nice moments: the warm embrace of a loved one; fine wine; Reese's peanut butter cups; discovering leftover pizza slices. But something about it doesn't sit right with you. Isn't it all just a bit too . . . artificial? Convenient? Unbelievable? *The Matrix*?

One evening, you climb into bed as usual but judder awake as a cloth bag is violently removed from your head. You are in a dark room. Sitting in front of you is Morpheus from *The Matrix*. "You are right," he says. "The world *is* a simulation. In fact, the movie *The Matrix* was a computer virus introduced into the real Matrix to try to awaken people to the possibility that they are living in a Matrix! Well done for figuring it out." Just as he does in the movie, he then opens his fists to reveal two pills: a red one and a blue one. "Blue returns you to your bed and all this will be forgotten. Red wakes you up in the 'real world' outside of the Matrix, but it's not pretty. There are no special powers. You are not the one. No Trinity awaits you. You can't flit between the two worlds."

Which would you pick? Is it better to live in an efficient lie or a harrowing truth?

You take the red pill, deciding for reality at all costs. You awake in a dark bunker, fifteen storeys below the ground. Morpheus was right—reality really isn't pretty. Everyone lives underground; you will never go "outside" again; the only thing to eat is a Soylent-style paste; Reese's Peanut Butter Cups are a distant, fading memory.

But you have the truth. Time passes. You try to make the best of this new world. Then, one night, you are kidnapped. You awake as a cloth bag is removed from your head, and you see, once more, Morpheus.

"Sorry," he begins. "Last time we met, I wasn't entirely truthful. This post-apocalyptic world is not the real world, either. You are still in the Matrix, just a post-apocalyptic version of it. A kind of reality halfway house. A simulation designed to warn you how bad actual "reality" really is. It is, like, really bad." Once again, he holds out the red pill and the blue pill. "Do you still want to see how deep the rabbit hole goes?"

What would you do this time? Accept this "reality halfway house" or go for truth, however brutal? And what if the next world Morpheus reveals to you isn't actually "reality" either? What if it's just another Matrix? What if what Neo discovered in the movie was just another simulation where he got to live out his "the one" fantasy, win the girl, and wear bitchin' leather?

TL;DR: Even if you escape the Matrix, you have no idea whether the world outside of it is just another Matrix. Quit while you're ahead. Which is exactly what they should have done after the first Matrix movie.

I Tweet Therefore I Am

Cogito, ergo sum: "I think, therefore I am." It's the $E=mc^2$ of philosophy. Everyone knows this phrase is important but few know why. At first glance, "I think, therefore I am" seems intuitively simple. But like a lot of philosophy, to appreciate its influence, you need to place it in its historical context. Throughout history, scepticism has been a constant in philosophy. Philosophical scepticism allows you to trample all over thoughts rather than try to build them up into coherent structures. It shows that all our senses are unreliable and all our concepts fallible—demolition being the sexier, simpler younger brother of construction.

Descartes wanted to contain radical scepticism. He set out to take the sceptics down a peg or two by proving that there must be some knowledge that's untouchable, even by the most extreme forms of scepticism. Descartes' road to certainty was paved as such.

1. Let's assume that there's an all-powerful evil demon controlling all our thoughts, manipulating everything we perceive of the world.
2. Accepting this demon exists, is there any way to prove something beyond all doubt? Would there be anything outside of the demon's control?
3. "I doubt it."
4. Well, if I doubt it, then I'm thinking, right? To doubt requires thought.
5. There is a part of me that the demon cannot trick—namely, my perception of my existence.
6. In conclusion, I think, therefore I am. Take that, sceptics (and evil demons)!

Archimedes, the Greek tinker, famously said, "Give me a lever long enough and a fulcrum on which to place it, and I shall move the world." Once Descartes established his one undoubtable truth, we had our fulcrum of knowledge upon which all the rest could be levered. We could push back the radical sceptics. Therefore, Descartes' simple sentence has prevailed, infamous, for hundreds of years.

TL;DR: The bad news? There might be an evil demon that controls all your thoughts. The good news? In order to be deceived by it, you must at least exist. The bad news of existence, however? *Taxes.*

Fact File: René Descartes

Influence: 5/10

Nationality: French

Dates: 1596 – 1650

Groupies: Immanuel Kant, Baruch Spinoza, dualists

·R. Cartesius·

Bio: Descartes is often regarded as the first modern philosopher. He lived in a time in which everything the Church said was, literally, gospel. Descartes set out to prove philosophy can give definitive answers to difficult questions, so we wouldn't need to rely on spirituality.

Greatest Idea: I think, therefore I am (aka *cogito, ergo sum*). This simple idea helped to spark the Enlightenment, which ultimately diminished the Catholic Church's control on the important questions of the day.

Worst Idea: Static cosmological fluid. In Descartes' time, most scientists already knew the earth revolved around the sun, but the Roman Catholic Church had a convincing method of opinion persuasion called burning people alive. So, fearing religious retaliation, Descartes refrained from publishing his work *Le Monde* in its original form. Instead, he softened his ideas to a compromise between geocentric and heliocentric theories, saying the cosmos was engulfed in a static fluid, and so while the earth did rotate around the sun, it was as a kind of cosmic afterthought.

Anecdote: In 1619, Descartes was struggling to decide whether to join the army or pursue a career in philosophy. One night he woke from a particularly vivid dream in which he opened a book and saw the title of poem called "What path of life should I choose?" Not being able to remember the rest of the poem, he concluded that since he dreamt about a book it had to be a sign to favour the scientific world over that of looting and conquering. It's less clear why he didn't see it as a sign to become a poet. Perhaps because he liked fame, money, and heating.

Quotes:

"The reading of all good books is like a conversation with the finest minds of past centuries." *With the advantage of being able to shut them up whenever you want.*

"Except our own thoughts, there is nothing absolutely in our power." *And even that isn't a given, if you're married.*

"If you would be a real seeker after truth, it is necessary that at least once in your life you doubt, as far as possible, all things." *Including this, which means everything is fine. Carry on . . .*

Descartes in Objects:

1. "Science . . . it works, bitches" poster: The seventeenth century was a time of scientific revolutions, and not a moment too soon, as far as he was concerned.

2. Medal: He served for four years in the army.

3: Eye mask: Due to "ill health" he never got out of bed in the morning. When he finally changed his regime, he contracted pneumonia and died within a year.

4: Censored book: His work was on the Vatican's list of prohibited works.

5. Rich man's clothes: He liked dressing up in fancy outfits.

6. Money: He was financially smart; he invested in bonds that gave him a regular income throughout life.

7. Clogs: He lived for more than twenty years in Holland, the time during which most of his work originated.

Pop-culture equivalent: The hipster. Both are bad in the morning, like to dress fancily, and mingle with arty people. He lived in Holland as the first coffee houses appeared. And if that weren't enough, he was also into meditation, long before it was cool. If he were still alive today he'd be riding a fixie, dressed in a lumberjack shirt, and telling people to "wake up" and "question things" all while trying to sell his self-published book of haiku poetry.

TL;DR: René Descartes is hugely important for having helped validate philosophy as a noble endeavour during a difficult time in which whatever the Church said was "fact". Unfortunately, they have never made free cookies a "fact". If they did, congregation numbers might be higher.

The Mind-Body Diet: How to Lose a Soul In Less than Two Weeks!

Another concept closely connected to René Descartes is the mind-body problem. It tries to answer this question: is the mind of the same substance as the body? To Descartes, post *cogito, ergo sum*, it seemed logical that they weren't, for while the body can be deceived by the evil demon, the soul and its "doubting I" can't be tricked. Hence, we must be made out of two separate substances:

1. A mind/consciousness/soul (immortal)

2. A physical body (very much mortal)

It remains a contentious idea. Some like the idea of a separation because it helps explain tricky problems, such as which part of us goes on to the afterlife (spoiler alert: the soul). Others reject the division because, well, there's simply no scientific evidence for it. And science hates unproven theories as much as you hate treading on Lego.

The arguers have split into two broad camps.

1. Dualists: Dualists believe there's a distinction between the physical and mental parts of existence.

Advantages — immortality (in one form or another).

Disadvantages — hard to explain how the nonphysical soul compels the physical body to do anything. Also, split body and mind and you can have . . . zombies. No one needs that.

2. Monists: For Monists there's only the physical world, which is governed by the laws of nature.

Advantages — less to explain. Fewer zombies.

Disadvantages — we're mortal, soulless, and need an explanation about whether mind or matter is the illusion fooling the other.

Most people tend to favour dualism, as it's even harder to find your soulmate if you don't believe in souls, and matter tends to get old and die (or at least needs expensive cosmetic surgery), a problem generally not attributed to souls.

TL;DR: If you believe there's a separation between the body and *you* (consciousness, personality, soul), you're a dualist. If you think it's just a clever trick of your very physical body, you're a monist. If you've no idea but want everyone to keep fighting about it, you're a duelist.

Got Soul?

So, the soul is a human construct, most likely conceived to bridge the gap between mortality and the afterlife. Fine. But then where is the soul located? How does it work? When does it enter the body? Does it enter the body? So many questions, so little time (not for souls—they're immortal). Here's a quick overview of how some of history's famous thinkers believed the soul worked.

1. Socrates and Plato: The soul has three parts—rationality (in the head); emotions (in the chest); and desires (in the stomach). "...our soul is immortal and never destroyed?"

2. Aristotle: The soul is our whole body. We're mortal. The soul enters our bodies at different points. "In the case of male children . . . on the fortieth day but if the child be a female . . . about the ninetieth day."

3. Buddha: No soul; no permanent essence. We're just a bundle of mental functions, and to overcome our misperception, we have to practice non-attachment and become aware of our default thought-to-thought intention-and-reaction loops. "Only through ignorance and delusion do men indulge in the dream that their souls are separate and self-existing entities."

4. René Descartes: It's the pineal gland, at the centre of the brain. "The reason I believe this is that I cannot find any part of the brain, except this, which is not double."

5. Polynesia: In some Polynesian religions, a sneeze is seen as a struggle between the person and soul. Confusingly, it can be both the soul leaving and fighting to re-enter the body.

6. Duncan MacDougall: No idea where it is, but it weighs twenty-one grams (hence the movie of the same name). "The soul's weight is removed from the body virtually at the instant of last breath, though in persons of sluggish temperament it may remain in the body for a full minute."

7. Bobby Byrd ft. James Brown: "I Know You Got Soul."

8. Nadya Yuguseva, a shaman from the Altai: "A woman has forty souls; men have just one." Which seems more plausible if we assume she's talking about footwear.

TL;DR: Many definitions and locations of the soul have been offered over the course of history. All we're sure about is that most people want one, and that our bosses have already sold theirs.

Got Consciousness?

What good is it to have a soul if you're not conscious? But wait, what's consciousness? Many people have tried to find out. But conveniently, no one knows, which means you can decide for yourself and never be wrong (for now). *Yay!* What type of consciousness believer are you?

You think that consciousness exists in its own separate realm, outside of reality = *You're a substance dualist*

You think consciousness is simply a brain function = *You're a functionalist*

You think consciousness is a physical part of matter, like electromagnetism = *You're a property dualist*

You think consciousness and our mental states are physical events you could see in a brain scan = *You're an identity theorist*

You think consciousness is a sensation that grows out of brain states = *You're an emergent dualist*

You think consciousness is just behaviour and we appear conscious because of how we behave = *You're a behaviourist*

You think consciousness is just thinking but on a higher level: thoughts^2 = *You're a higher-order theorist*

You think consciousness is the sensation of your most significant thoughts being highlighted = *You're a cognitivist*

You think consciousness is best enjoyed rather than theorised =
You're a normal person

TL;DR: There are many fancy labels you can give yourself based on where you believe consciousness comes from, from behaviourist to substance dualist. No matter where you believe it comes from, look up from your phone while crossing the road, or you might lose it.

The Chinese (Bath)room

While there's debate about whether we have souls, we're all aware that we're conscious, and that our particular type of consciousness is a big part of what makes humans special (that and opposable thumbs). But what if a machine became conscious in the same way as we are (briefly, after four strong coffees)? Would it deserve the same rights as we do?

Before answering this question, let's step back a second. Can machines be knowledgeable and intelligent? "Knowledge" is often used as a synonym for "intelligence," while it's more accurate to say that intelligence is what you display when you use knowledge correctly:

Knowledge + knowing how to use it = intelligence (e.g. parents are out tonight + knowing to how send a message to your entire phone book = awesome house party that gets you grounded for a month).

This seems to make intuitive sense, but then try this thought experiment from philosopher John Searle. If you're not on it already, picture yourself sitting on your toilet. Now, imagine someone slides a piece of paper under the bathroom door. You pick up that piece of paper and see that it has Chinese characters on it. You don't understand Mandarin, so you have no idea what's written on the paper. But then you discover that your beloved, dog-eared copy of *Fast Philosophy* has been replaced with a giant instruction book. This book allows you to look up the string of Mandarin characters on the note you received, and it will tell you what Mandarin character string you should write to reply to it.

You follow the book's instructions, writing out what you hope is the correct Mandarin response, and slide it back under the door. A few second later, you get a reply. You still have no idea what the topic of the conversation is, who's in your house, or why they're writing to you in Mandarin. Still, you keep at it. Matching. Writing. Sliding.

Now, imagine that while you know what's going on in the room, the person on the other side of the door, writing you these notes, does not. If your instruction manual is perfect, as are the notes you're passing out, wouldn't that person conclude you're an intelligent Mandarin speaker?

Yet, you aren't. You are, in effect, acting just like a computer program. Instructions tell you how to use input. You compare this input against an array and deliver an output. Your job is merely pattern matching. Which leads us to the next question: if a machine did this process instead of you, could it be said that this machine is intelligent? How can you test for *true* intelligence compared to "machine intelligence"?

TL;DR: The Chinese room thought experiment shows that what from the outside looks like intelligence can be nothing more than pattern matching. It's a fine line between human and machine intelligence, and all we know for sure is only one of the two needs toilet breaks.

What's Intelligence Got to Do with It?

The distinction between knowledge and intelligence is important because we're more inclined to accept that a computer program holds knowledge than to say it's intelligent. There is a quality to intelligence that we tend to want to reserve for humans.

Enigma code breaker Alan Turing famously said that if a computer can convince a human that it's communicating with another human, it can be said to be intelligent. This became the Turing test, through which artificial intelligence (AI) programmes are put through their paces answering human-created, tricky, stupid, and ambiguous questions, such as Epimenides' liar's paradox, the statement: "This sentence is false" (a contradiction because if the sentence is false, it's true; if the sentence is true, it's also false).

These types of questions are confusing enough for us to answer intelligently, and very hard for a machine (whether in a bathroom or not) to convincingly fake an intelligent response to. When a machine passes the Turing test, it will be a huge deal in the media. Many people think we're already close to building truly conscious machines. Which could potentially be the last invention ever made by humans. Intelligent machines that aren't bound by physical constraints would transcend us, leaving us no chance to ever catch up.

For John Searle, the Chinese room was supposed to be the antidote to this AI hype. He believes that blindly following a process which, by chance, involves the correct use of Mandarin doesn't show intelligence (just as you can kick a football once without being a footballer, or use a toilet without understanding how sewers work). Simulated intelligence is not real intelligence. This distinction is pivotal. If the computer doesn't understand what it's doing, it cannot be considered intelligent. He thus divided AI into two types:

1. Strong AI – the computer has a mind in the same sense that human beings have minds
2. Weak AI – the computer simulates having intelligence, regardless of how successful this simulation is and whether it outperforms humans on a task or not

At best, the computer in the Chinese room might be considered weak AI. But we've created nothing even close to resembling strong AI. Which is perhaps unsurprising, as we're still unsure how our own brains and consciousness work. We still don't know if there's even a unique, emergent quality to consciousness. It might be nothing more than millions of simultaneous processes in the brain merely convincing us consciousness is something special. Just like in Searle's Chinese room.

Perhaps one day we will build a machine that is conscious. If we do, and you're a dualist, and so believe in souls, you'll have a new, interesting problem—you'll have to argue why something can be conscious and not have a soul, or else accept that machines now have them, too.

TL;DR: The Turing test and the Chinese bathroom show us that consciousness is still poorly understood. Fortunately, at least intelligence is well distributed (no one has ever complained about having too little of it).

CHAPTER 8

RATIONALISM AND EMPIRICISM

Reasoning Is Elementary, My Dear Watson (and Sherlock)

After a woman's dead body is discovered in her apartment, two famous sleuths are sent to try to identify the murderer. One is famous detective Sherlock Holmes, the other his resourceful sidekick, Dr. Watson. They enter the apartment, survey the crime scene, and analyse it, each using his own favoured method.

"Once again, I've solved the case, Watson," says Sherlock. Watson smiles.

"Possible, but it's more likely that in this instance, I have the correct conclusion, Sherlock!"

"Okay, you go first then," says Sherlock.

"Well, we both know that the first step in solving a case is to observe the crime scene. The front door is intact, which implies the victim knew the killer. Observing the blood-splatter pattern, I can *deduce* that the murder weapon is an axe. The next-door neighbour is a lumberjack—it says it right on his doorbell. In my experience, most lumberjacks use axes. The murderer is, therefore, most certainly the next-door neighbour."

"Well," says Sherlock, "interesting, but not elementary, my dear Watson. For can experience not be quite misleading? Is it not better to start with a general truth and test it against one's evidence? It is a general fact of criminal statistics that most young attractive females get killed by their ex-boyfriends. As you correctly observed, from the door and the wounds, in this case, it does appear the victim knew her killer. But rather than deducing that it is the neighbour, I *infer* that the ex-boyfriend is the culprit."

It's a stalemate. Neither backs down, but since Watson's theory involves less walking, they head next door, where they interrogate the neighbour, who quickly confesses. Watson was right. But during the interrogation, they learn that the neighbour is, in fact, also the ex-boyfriend. One used deduction to get his answer, and the other used induction. Both were correct.

TL;DR: There are multiple modes of reasoning. The big two are deduction (from general rule to instance, top down) and induction (instance to rule, bottom up). Crime scenes are a bit like art-house horror movies; there are multiple ways to interpret them, and while something always gets murdered, too often it's just good taste.

The Blank Slate of Innate Ideas

Epistemology is the branch of philosophy concerned with how knowledge works. Two opposing factions became especially polarised in regards to this philosophy during the eighteenth century.

1. **Rationalists**: Knowledge is discovered via deduction. From law to instance.

THEORY   HYPOTHESIS   OBSERVATION   CONFIRMATION

Rationalism is a top-down approach working from abstract universal principles down to the confirmation of everyday examples. Theory over practice.

Rationalists believe there is innate knowledge. Our senses can help us to unravel truths that exist independent of experience, such as the mathematical truth that all triangles have three sides. If we understand the concept, we understand the law. Of course, for deduction to work you need correct universal principles from which you can deduce—just as a GPS does you no good, no matter how accurate it is, if your friends give you the wrong address for the party. Plato, Descartes, and Spinoza are famous rational thinkers.

2. **Empiricists:** Knowledge is created via induction. From instance to law.

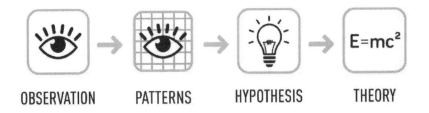

OBSERVATION   **PATTERNS**   **HYPOTHESIS**   **THEORY**

It's a bottom-up approach leading from individual examples to the formulation of a general law. Practice over theory.

All knowledge is derived from experience alone, argued British thinkers Locke, Berkeley, and Hume, the most famous proponents of empiricism. We start as blank slates and via the impressions we get through our senses, we reason, and thus create knowledge. Science is mostly founded on empiricist principles that see us improve our theories via empirical observations. For induction to work you have to be able to trust your senses, which, as anyone who's gotten drunk and tried to pole-vault over a wall can tell you, sometimes only lead you to err and ER.

TL;DR: Philosophy is divided over whether the cool logic of deduction or the fundamental observations of experience are better. For empiricist Francis Bacon, the answer was obvious: "Empiricists are like ants; they collect and put to use; but rationalists are like spiders; they spin threads out of themselves."

Fact File: David Hume

Influence: 6/10

Nationality: Scottish

Dates: 1711 – 1776

Groupies: Immanuel Kant, Arthur Schopenhauer, Karl Popper, John Locke

Bio: An influential Scottish philosopher and proponent of empiricism and scepticism. Regarded by some as the greatest English-language philosopher of all time for contributions as a historian, essayist, diplomat, and economist.

Greatest Idea: Hume's fork. Only two kinds of truth-claims exist:

1. Statements about ideas. These are analytical and knowable without sense experience, e.g. definitions such as "a person who is blind can't see".
2. Statements about the world. These are synthetical and need experience to be validated, e.g. "people who are blind suck at bird-watching".

Unfortunately, knowledge gets stuck on both prongs. Statements about the world cannot be trusted since our senses can trick us. Ideas seem safer but can't be proven, as they rely on being correctly defined.

Worst Idea: *A Treatise of Human Nature*. Now considered his most important book, it was far from a crowd pleaser when first published. The reception was so bad, in fact, that Hume said the book "fell dead-born from the press, without reaching such distinctions even to excite a murmur among the zealots". So, he sold out (philosophy style) by writing a much simpler version of it—*An Enquiry Concerning Human Understanding*. Despite still sounding really boring, it did hit the zeitgeist (although probably not as much as *The Enquiry Effect: You will not believe what happened when this English philosopher discovered a theory too radical to be allowed!* would have).

Anecdote: Hume was openly critical of the Church. One day, while out walking, he fell into a swamp and found himself sinking rapidly. He shouted for help drawing the attention of a woman. "Are ne ye Hume the Atheist?" she said. "Yes. But does not Christian charity command you to do good to everyone?" Hume replied. "Christian charity here, Christian charity there," said the woman dismissively. "I'll do nothing for you till ye turn a Christian yourself, repeat the Lord's Prayer and the Creed, or I'll let ye grafe there as I fand ye." Afraid for his life, Hume did as he was told, was freed, and somehow resisted the urge to push the woman in afterwards.

Quotes:

"The life of man is of no greater importance to the universe than that of an oyster." *Probably less, actually, since at least oysters have the decency to be delicious.*

"Beauty is no quality in things themselves: it exists merely in the mind which contemplates them; and each mind perceives a different beauty." *This might be true but makes for a terrible pick-up line.*

"A wise man proportions his belief to the evidence." *An even wiser man weighs the evidence down with concrete and throws it off the nearest bridge.*

Hume in Objects:

1. Powdered wig: Hume studied law but later said it made him nauseous.

2. Clown nose: It is said that he had an impeccable talent for entertaining audiences.

3. Prescription drugs: As a young man, Hume was so obsessed with finding the "real truth" that he had a nervous breakdown.

4. Diploma: A smart child, he entered university at the age of twelve.

5. European flag: His teachings first caught on in Europe and only later made him famous in Britain.

6. Pop-culture equivalent: Gandalf from *The Lord of the Rings*. Both travelled on stately errands. Like Gandalf, Hume was exceptionally smart and a beloved friend of many factions. The influence of both, in their realms, was formidable. While Gandalf mostly influenced Hobbits, Hume worked his magic on his own diminutive pair— Rousseau and Kant. Kant went as far as to say that Hume's work awoke him from a "slumber of prejudice". Which sounds bad but still involves slumber and so was probably not all that shabby.

TL;DR: Hume forked knowledge into two categories: statements about ideas (necessarily true by logic but uninformative about the world) and statements about the world (which can't be proven). Meaning his fork is both disappointing and completely useless for eating spaghetti.

Ockham's Razor: Giving Ideas a Clean Cut
Since the Middle Ages

As you know, life can be pretty complicated. It isn't always clear what you should believe, when it's appropriate to believe the worst, and why the worst always happens to you. Luckily, philosophy has your back—in particular, William of Ockham and his special, metaphorical razor. The principle simply states that if you can't decide between multiple hypotheses, pick the explanation that contains the fewest assumptions.

The following table explains this, as well as some of Ockham's other, less known (because we're making them up), utensils.

Utensil	Situation	Definition	Without Utensil	With Utensil
Ockham's razor	You hear a loud bump coming from the attic.	If you can't decide between multiple hypotheses, choose the one that requires the fewest assumptions.	OMG THERE'S A MONSTER IN THE ATTIC HITTING THE HEATING PIPE! I hope it's vegetarian.	The heating pipe made a noise.
Ockham's chastity belt	You are accused of infidelity.	If you want to have sex with multiple people, it's best to get amnesia afterwards (especially if you're the president).	"Yeah, I pretty much had a lot of sex with that woman. Including weird stuff with cigars."	"I did not have sexual relations with that woman."
Ockham's firewall	A Nigerian prince emails you offering you millions of dollars.	If it sounds too good to be true, it's a Nigerian prince.	Say goodbye to your identity and your inheritance.	Report spam.
Ockham's cleaver	Your country has a resource shortage.	If you want to invade a country for its natural resources, hold good press conferences.	"Iraq has a lot of oil and we'd kind of like some of it, and we've got this big army anyway and so it sort of feels like we should do something with it, you know?"	"Iraq has weapons of mass destruction."
Ockham's stethoscope	You need to create demand for a dangerous product.	If you want to say something nonsensical, first put on a white jacket.	"Smoking is fun but will kill you (even if you're a doctor)."	"More doctors smoke Camels than any other cigarette!"

TL;DR: Ockham's razor says, when weighing up multiple possibilities, always go with the hypothesis that contains the fewest assumptions. Assumptions are to hypotheses what back hair is to people: less is more.

An Unbiased Tour of Biases

It's not only fear of monsters in the attic that can make us giddily irrational. Here's a tour of some of the more comical, underrated cognitive biases. Hopefully once you know their names, you'll better be able to notice them, and so will be less likely to fall victim to any of them.

The Cheerleader Effect: The tendency for people to appear more attractive in a group than in isolation. *He must be handsome—look at all his friends.*

The Hindsight Bias: The tendency to think the things that have already happened were predictable. *Yeah, well, I guess it's only logical that at some point a lottery winner will also be struck by lightning, and have a piano fall on her head, at the same time, on Friday the thirteenth. After all, there are a lot of people in the world, and also pianos."*

The IKEA Effect: The tendency to be more emotionally attached to things you've built, even if you just screwed the legs on. *This apple pie that I've baked, from frozen is really very delicious (in hindsight)!*

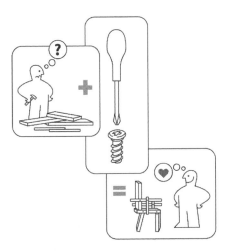

The Illusion of Control: The tendency to overestimate the influence we have over external events. *My prayers are the best vaccination you could ever ask for!*

Information Bias: The tendency to want information even when it cannot affect our actions. *Tell me again about all those cognitive biases! They're really fun (and under my control, with their legs on, in hindsight!).*

Post-Purchase Rationalisation: The tendency to rationalise a purchase as a good investment. *I just knew buying* Fast Philosophy *was a good idea. It's smart, funny and its authors handsome (in a very large group).*

The Dunning-Kruger Effect: The inability for incompetent people to know they are incompetent because they can't tell the difference between competence and incompetence based on their limited knowledge. *Couldn't happen to me, I'm extremely competent in my analysis of my own competence!*

TL;DR: In hindsight, in a group, you are competent and attractive and everything is under your control, as long as you assembled some of it and are too uninformed to know how long before that bit falls off.

Rhetorical Fail-acies

A philosopher who never takes part in a debate is like a boxer who never enters the ring. The strongest attack is a good defence, so learn to spot these rhetorical fallacies, slips of logic, misdirections of meaning, and obfuscations of fact.

APPEALING TO THE INTELLECT

For the argument: German philosophers are the best.

Authorities: "Over four hundred of the best footballers agreed, Aristotle is their favourite Greek restaurant."

Common practice: "In German taverns, everyone talks philosophy, so of course Germans are the best philosophers."

Money: "The wealthiest philosophers all come from Germany."

Ignorance: "I don't know of a single German philosopher who isn't amazing."

Tradition: "German philosophers were the most influential philosophers in the nineteenth and twentieth centuries, so they must be now, too, in the twenty-first century."

APPEALING TO SENTIMENTS

For the argument: The best philosopher is a *Fast* Philosopher.

Fear: "People who aren't *Fast* Philosophers have a much shorter life expectancy."

Flattery: "Someone as intelligent as you already knows why."

Ridicule: "Believing that traditional philosophy is better than *Fast Philosophy* is like believing in Santa Claus and chocolate unicorns."

Consequence of belief: "You bought this book, and you're not the kind of person who wastes money on an inferior education."

FAULTY DEDUCTIONS

For the argument: It's fine I spent all our money on magic beans.

Anecdotes as evidence: "I read a story about a boy who spent his money on magic beans. He had giant fun."

Design fallacy: "The beans cost exactly the amount of money I had left. That must be a sign they were the right thing to buy."

Gambler's fallacy: "The last five lots of magic beans didn't work, so it's definitely time for my luck to change."

False middle ground: "You wanted me to buy bread; I wanted to set the money on fire in a elaborate protest against capitalism. Magic beans are a fair compromise."

MANIPULATION OF THE MESSAGE

For the argument: You should vote for me."

Lie: "My opponent's favourite hobby is clubbing baby seals to death."

Red herring: "Thanks for asking this. It reminds me of a story from last summer. A cute puppy . . ."

Confirmation bias: "The first page of Google results about me is all really positive."

False dilemma: "Either I win or the terrorists win. And we can't risk that."

Biased generalisation: "A poll of my friends proved I'm the most popular candidate."

DIRECT ATTACKS

For the argument: *Fast Philosophy* is not a waste of time.

Ad hominem: "Anyone who attacks *Fast Philosophy* is a hatemonger."

Burden of proof: "No one has been able to show me that it is. Prove it."

Genetic fallacy: "Well, of course the intellectual liberal media is going to say that philosophy is useless."

Guilt by association: "Of course you wouldn't want to educate children in *Fast Philosophy*; a terrorist wouldn't, either."

Straw man: "Saying that the humanities offer no value to the economy is like saying all philosophers should be yoga teachers."

LIBERTIES OF CAUSE AND EFFECT

For the argument: The government should provide every citizen with a copy of *Fast Philosophy*.

Circular logic: "Education is important. *Fast Philosophy* educates. Therefore, if you don't think *Fast Philosophy* should be distributed to everyone, you are against education."

Two wrongs make a right: "Spending tax money on eighty million copies of a book is wrong, but so is spending it on weapons research and war. In the end, it's the lesser of two evils."

Ignoring common cause: "Ever since *Fast Philosophy* came out the economy has grown; therefore, the more people read it, the more the economy will improve."

Affirming the consequent: "Reading philosophy books gives you broader vocabularies, so you've obviously read a lot of philosophical books."

TL;DR: Arguing is a bit like football; unless the referee blows the whistle, it isn't a foul.

Fact File: Immanuel Kant

Influence: 10/10

Nationality: Prussian

Dates: 1724 – 1804

Groupies: Pretty much everyone. He's so famous he even has a whole school of thought named after him: Kantianism.

Bio: Kant's funny name (at least for English speakers) and his unusual personal habits have somewhat stolen the focus from his achievements (such as almost single-handedly ending the rationalism vs. empiricism debate). He was mostly interested in questions of metaphysics: Is there a god? What is existence? Are we free? What can we know about the things we can't see or prove?

Greatest Idea: Copernican revolution. This term generally describes the paradigm shift from the geocentric to the heliocentric model of the solar system. But it's also used as a metaphor for Kant's new approach to philosophy. Traditionally, philosophers put the external world with its objects at the centre of inquiry. Kant's revolutionary idea was to reverse this and not ask how the world and its objects are constituted but, instead, what conditions make it possible for us to have knowledge of the world, thus putting the subject at the centre.

Worst Idea: Kant made it a religious convention to seal the blinds of his bedroom as tight as possible. He believed that bedbugs were caused by fresh air and light streaming into his room, which was both a silly notion and counterproductive. It's more likely that the infestation was caused by the negligence of his servant, Lampe, who struggled with an alcohol addiction for many years.

Anecdote: Kant is one of history's most peculiar men, and there are dozens of anecdotes about his eccentric behaviour. If you've seen the movie *Groundhog Day*, you've a pretty good idea what it was like to be him. His days were planned to precision—each began at 5am with his servant thundering the same words: "It is time!" His only meal of the day was lunch, which always lasted precisely three hours, from one to four. The meal had at least two guests but never more than five. Kant would then walk the same street of his home-town, Königsberg, exactly eight times, no matter the weather. Over the course of his entire adult life, Kant only missed or delayed these walks a handful of times. It is said that every time this occurred the people of Königsberg altered their clocks, thinking it was more likely they were wrong than Kant was off schedule.

Quotes:

"*Sapere aude*! Have courage to use your own reason!" *And even more courage to ignore it when it tells you to drunkenly text your ex.*

"By a lie, a man . . . annihilates his dignity as a man." *And by getting caught in his lie, his dignity as a scoundrel.*

"Thoughts without content are empty; intuitions without concepts are blind." *But blind intuition is great fun and always leaves you content.*

Kant in Objects:

1. Milky Way poster: His first work was a well-received treaty about cosmic clusters.

2. Books by Descartes and Hume: These represent the rivalling theories that he helped to consolidate (rationalism and empiricism).

3. Best Teacher Award: He was very popular with his students.

4. Home mat: He never travelled.

5. A stool: He was very short.

6. Pop-culture equivalent: Superman. Just like Superman, Kant was

led strongly by his sense of duty. Superman got this from his small-town upbringing, as did Kant, who was a local boy at heart and barely ever left his hometown. Duty restricted Superman; hyper-rationality restricted Kant. Both Superman's and Kant's powers were so tremendous that they were unfathomable to others. Philosophy is divided in epochs—"the Greeks", "the Romans", etc. The only thinker regularly used as an epoch himself is Kant. Any budding *Fast* Philosopher can show his or her prowess by casually dropping "after Kant" or "before Kant" into conversations.

TL:DR: Kant was a quirky Prussian philosopher who was so influential an entire school of thought was named after him. Kant's revolutionary idea was to put the subject at the centre of philosophical enquiry, not the world. You've probably met a few people who have taken this too far, making themselves the only subject in the entire world. They are, in several ways, Kants.

Knowledge: It's Complicated – Kant's Synthetic A Priori

How do we acquire knowledge? Through experience or the understanding of truths? Kant's breakthrough insight was to reformulate the problem in such a way that rationalism and empiricism weren't mutually exclusive theories anymore, but instead two sides of the same coin. To understand Kant's twist on the original question, we'll have to discuss the distinctions between analytical/synthetical and a priori/a posteriori knowledge. Unfortunately, there's no sugarcoating this topic. It's one of philosophy's most demanding concepts. Grasp it and you will be ahead of most students who study philosophy full-time.

Essentially, there are two basic types of knowledge:

1. A priori = propositions we can justify without experience, e.g. "7 x 7 = 49" or "All bachelors are unmarried". What a bachelor is doesn't depend on various bachelors; it's already contained in its own definition (i.e. a bachelor must be unmarried to be a bachelor).
2. A posteriori = propositions we can justify only with experience. For example: "It rains a lot in England" or "The rents are too damn high in San Francisco".

Okay so far? Great. It's really just a reformulation of the original controversy: is experience or reasoning more important for knowledge?

Next, Kant added another distinction to knowledge, further subdividing it into analytic and synthetic propositions:

1. Analytic = a proposition which is trying to explain a concept that is contained in the subject, e.g. "all triangles have three sides". Triangles already contain the concept of sides and three. Analytic statements point inwards, towards themselves.
2. Synthetic = a proposition that references something not already contained in itself, e.g. "all creatures with hearts also have kidneys". The proposition doesn't reference itself but points outwards to something else (since the concept of a heart doesn't include kidneys).

Combine these distinctions and you get the following four possible combinations, arranged here in a matrix. The four cases represent all possible modes of knowledge that arise from mixing the distinction of reference (analytic vs. synthetic) with the justification (a priori vs. a posteriori).

PROPOSITION	A priori (no experience needed for validation)	A posteriori (validated with experience)
Analytic (inward; predicate contains subject)	**Analytic a priori** = All bachelors are unmarried. *Things we know because we defined them. Simple and boring. Think of this as the place where all definitions live. Rationalists emphasise this type of knowledge as the true form of knowledge.*	**Analytic a posteriori** = n/a. *Doesn't exist, as it is a logical fallacy. Experience can't validate something that is already true by definition.*
Synthetic (outward; predicate does not contain subject)	**Synthetic a priori** = All metaphysical questions. *The place where all the magic happens. The most fundamental and interesting questions about the universe and our existence fall into this category. Questions of this type are normally referred to as metaphysical questions: What are the laws of nature? Does God exist? Is causality real or an illusion? etc.*	**Synthetic a posteriori** = Rain is wet. Toast always falls butter-side down. *Propositions that are not self-referential and thus must be justified through experience. Simple and boring. Basically all the stuff we know that isn't a definition. Empiricists hold that this type of knowledge is prime.*

What makes synthetic a priori questions so interesting?

1. They increase our understanding. Being synthetic, they reference something that isn't already conceptually contained in the question, broadening our understanding of the world.
2. They are necessarily and universally true (since anything a priori cannot be falsified by experience).

What can be possibly be better than knowledge that both expands your understanding and can never be proven wrong? Kant showed any metaphysical judgement must be synthetic a priori; otherwise, it's either uninformative or unjustifiable. Consolidating rationalism and empiricism in this way, by showing the deeper structure of knowledge, is the great achievement of Kant's *Critique of Pure Reason*.

TL;DR: Kant showed that the most interesting questions are metaphysical: questions about things we can't know intuitively or prove by experience and are therefore synthetic a priori. If people understand you when you quote that last sentence, don't get into an argument with them.

CHAPTER 9

MORALITY AND UTOPIA

Is It Always Wrong to Kill?

You are Batman.

Congratulations! But don't spin yourself dizzy testing out your cape just yet because what's that ringing? That's right, it's the bat phone. It's police commissioner Gordon, who tells you to come to Gotham station as soon as possible—the Joker is there and has taken hostages.

Holy hot dogs, Batman! To the Batmobile!

When you arrive at Gotham station, you discover that the Joker is driving a speeding train out of Gotham central station, racing towards five railways workers he's tied to the train tracks. At first glance, there's nothing you can do to save them. But then you notice a nearby switch—if you flick this switch, the train will turn onto a secondary track, where one railway employee is busy working, oblivious to his peril. He will be killed instantly. There's no other way to stop the train. No secret weapon you can use in your tool belt. You can either do nothing and five people will die, or flip the switch and one will die.

What do you do, caped crusader? Flick the switch?

You might have come across this problem before in one guise or another; it's called the trolley problem. When it's presented to people like this, approximately 95 percent say they would flip the switch. Now let's make it a bit harder. The switch is disabled. But standing on a bridge is an overweight man. You calculate that his immense weight would stop the train. If you wanted to, you could push the man onto the track. This would save both the five people and the one person on the other track but kill him.

Would you push him? If not, why not? Does the pushing make it worse?

For most people it does. It's murder, isn't it? Not indirect murder through consequences, like flipping a switch. Let's go back to the original problem then. Five people are tied to one track, one on the other. You have a switch. But the five people are all at least eighty years old, and the one person, on the other track, is just fifteen.

Flip the switch and divert the train?

Welcome to the runaway train that is ethics—the branch of philosophy that tries to teach us how to act, or how to moralise how we didn't.

TL;DR: Morality is complicated. Small changes in the situation can quickly change what we perceive as right or wrong. Being Batman is hard; with great power comes great power bills.

The Trolley Problem — Running Over Morals

The trolley problem, like so much of philosophy, teases interesting questions out of us without offering immediate answers of absolution. In case you need help, here's how some of the big isms and countries would approach the trolley conundrum.

Hedonism: Riding this train is damn fun. Wait, what was the question?

Nihilism: Whichever you pick, those lucky bastards!

Apathy: I really couldn't care less.

Modern-day apathy: I might post a few of the crash pictures on Instagram.

Pessimism: If I try to flip the switch, I'll probably just break it and make everything worse and we'll all DIE AND THEN ARGH!

Feminism: Who's driving the train? The Joker? A man?! Well, isn't that just typical.

Chauvinism: Yeah, but women drove him to it.

Utilitarianism: Flip the switch. One is less than five.

America: This runaway train is an act of terrorism! Bomb the entire train station.

North Korea: What's a train and when exactly did the Dear Leader invent it?

Amtrak: Don't worry, if the train is supposed to arrive now, it won't turn up for another hour.

Russia: In Russia, switch flips you.

China: Train, what train? Everyone is fine. Stop asking difficult questions.

Communism: That's everyone's train. Someone else deal with it.

Capitalism: This train is too big to crash! The government has to bail it out.

Psychopathy: Why are you asking me? I'm driving the train. *Tchooo, tchooo!*

TL;DR: You don't have to filter the trolley problem through different isms to realise how little you want to be in the path of an oncoming train, no matter the switches. It's always better to lose your train of thought than your train.

The Utilitarian (Cookie) Monster

When confronted with the trolley problem, most people revert to what philosophers call utilitarianism: when in doubt, do whatever benefits the most people. Flip the switch. Kill one, save five. It's just logical, rational, simple maths. But is utilitarianism really such a silver bullet?

Take off your cape and replace it with a white jacket. You're now a nice, friendly doctor. In front of you lie five critically ill people who need organ transplants today or they'll die. You do not have those organs. But in the room next door you've just removed the tonsils of a young, healthy man. He's still unconscious, and you could remove his organs and use them to save the lives of these five people. *One for five.* Just like the trolley problem.

What do you do this time?

Most likely you flicked the switch in the trolley problem, but now you're appalled by the idea of harvesting organs. Yet, how is it any different beyond your having to take a more active role in "the one's" demise? Utilitarianism implores you to kill that man, doesn't it? Remember our old buddy maths? Utilitarianism seemed like such a neat solution then. How has it run out of control?

Swap the white jacket for a tailored suit and tie. You're the president of a brand-new country, Utilitarianland, which you've divided into ten states. Accordingly, you divide all the nation's resources and wealth equally by ten, adjusting a little based on the population size of each state. Great job so far, Dear Leader.

Five years later, the leaders of the ten states return to you to renegotiate the amount of country's tax revenues to be allocated to them. To your surprise, you see that although all received equal money five years ago, how each state has fared is vastly different. Nine have done okay, but one state, Utilifornia, has done much better than the others. Its economy is thriving, and its development is faster than that of all the other states combined. For every $1.00 you've given it, it has returned $2.50 of sweet, sweet tax income. The other states are lucky to even return $1.10; some simply lose money. Utilifornia's leader argues, therefore, that her state deserves much more investment than the other states. Is she right? Would you give it to her?

It would benefit the most people in the long run, creating more tax income to share. However, allocate more resources to Utilifornia and will it not use that investment to get yet further ahead of the other states? Which means in five years, using the same logic, it would justify an even large slice of the investment pie. You will stay loyal to utilitarianism but none of the other states will have the chance to catch up. Inadvertently, you will create what philosopher Robert Nozick called a utility monster.

Utilitarianism sounds good and is often confused with egalitarianism (treating everyone and everything equally). But utilitarianism only looks at numbers—not karma, not justice, not equality, not liberty. Should quantity always beat quality? And how do we quantify quality, happiness, or utility anyway?

TL;DR: Utilitarianism sounds logical, but it's easy to get so hung up on quantity that you forget to think about quality. Besides, some qualities resist quantification. It's easy to quantify income but hard to quantify contentment (and impossible to have the latter if your neighbour has more of the former).

Ethics, aka Being Morally Wrong No Matter What

If you've waited in a long line at the post office, read *Lord of the Flies*, or watched any game show staged on a deserted island, you know how thin the crust of civilisation is. As soon as someone gets delayed on the way to work, is shown a large enough cash prize, or becomes the tiniest little bit starving, all bets are off. "Any society is only three square meals away from revolution," Leon Trotsky wisely said.

Philosophers have categorised our efforts to contain our savagery into two main categories of normative ethics.

1. **Deontology.** *Rules, not outcomes.*

Since so many of the consequences of our actions are out of our hands, how do we know if we're living ethically? Deontology solves this neatly by stating that we should be judged only by whether we adhered to the rules we prescribed ourselves—whether it's the Ten Commandments, the golden rule, sharia law, or Scout law—regardless of the outcome.

Pros: Simple. Clear. Unambiguous. Neat outsourcing of responsibility.

Cons: Inflexible. Unclear what to do when there aren't defined rules. The Bible was explicit on what we should and shouldn't eat for dinner, but much vaguer on whether it's okay to use our smartphones during it.

2. **Consequentialism.** *Outcomes, not rules.*

Consequentialism says an act is only as good as the results it begets. Its followers argue that blindly following rules is the root of some of the worst atrocities ever committed. Therefore, we must look at the outcome of our actions and judge ethicality based on them.

Pros: Flexible. No need to learn lots of rules. Encourages self-reflection and responsibility.

Cons: Consequences are open to interpretation. Consequences for whom? You? Your family? Your nation? Dung beetles? We're bad at anticipating consequences even on short timescales. Just ask the person hugging the toilet the morning after a big night out.

TL;DR: There are two main approaches to ethics: deontology (following rules) and consequentialism (obsessing over outcomes). Tragically, ethics almost always gets in the way of following your obsessions.

Fact File: Karl Marx

· K. Marx ·

Influence: 9/10

Nationality: German

Dates: 1818 – 1883

Groupies: Who's who despots: Stalin, Mao, Pol Pot, and Castro

Bio: Karl Marx was a German philosopher who wrote mainly about the ongoing class struggle between the bourgeois and prole-tariat. In his opinion, history should be viewed not from the perspective of individuals but factions. After his death, many of his ideas were bent and twisted to the whims of various autocratic leaders.

Greatest Idea: Marxism. He analysed the endless class struggle of the bourgeoisie and the proletariat—a conflict he said was created by capitalism's alienation of workers who don't own what they produce. This degrades them to become mere means to an end, while the capital owners get disproportionately wealthy. He foresaw a socialist revolution, and hoped that it would end class struggle altogether since, following it, there would be no more class divisions.

Worst Idea: Marxism. It is said that the biggest tragedy of the twentieth century is the fact that it wasn't possible to test commu-nism on mice first. Marx, for better or worse, did not live to see the barbaric manner in which his ideas were implemented in various countries. He was convinced that a revolution by the proletariat, the class that had suffered so much during the industrial revolution, would lead to a fairer society. But the fundamental truth is that, given enough ideological rope, we always find a damn good reason to hang one another.

Anecdote: At a social event, a friend of Marx asked the philosopher who would clean Marx's boots if socialism took over. Slightly aggravated, Marx responded: "You should!" After the gathering dissolved, the man's wife said, "My dear Marx, I can't picture you in a socially levelled world, as you exhibit aristocratic tendencies." Marx replied, "Me neither. The time will come, but we have to be gone by then." Allegedly he once attended a conference for Marxists but left early saying if these people were Marxists he no longer wanted to be one.

Quotes:

"The philosophers have only interpreted the world in various ways; the point, however, is to change it." *In order to change anything, you have to have a concept of what to change it into, meaning you have to interpret the world differently, which is called philosophy. Therefore, there is no change without philosophy. Still you'll find this quote at many political rallies, but then politics and contradiction have never been mutually exclusive.*

"Religion is the opium of the masses." *At least it was, until they discovered Oreos, Netflix, and clickbait.*

"The realm of freedom actually begins only where labour which is determined by necessity and mundane considerations ceases." *Funnily enough, the right to be fired also begins exactly at the point where work ceases.*

Marx in Objects:

1. Fraternity sign: During his studies, Marx was a social butterfly and his father once had to bail him out of debt.

2. An issue of the *Neue Rheinische Zeitung*: Marx and Engels first published this newspaper to condemn the precarious situation of workers in Europe.

3. No Marxist sign: (see anecdote).

4. Shares: Because Marx earned little as a journalist, and even less as a philosopher, for a while he became a share trader.

5. Calendar: Marx was great with deadlines, submitting the manuscript for *Das Kapital* a mere sixteen years late.

Pop-culture equivalent: Che Guevara. Both had their reputations distorted after their deaths yet remain pop-culture figures, receivers of misguided admiration. Both remain influential, yet few know what they really stood for. Both had beards. Beards add historical heft, which is always useful for selling T-shirts.

TL;DR: Karl Marx was a German philosopher famous for his idea that society is divided into two warring factions—the bourgeoisie and the proletariat. While he wanted these to be equal, mostly his ideas were used by evil people to do awful things that both increased inequality and T-shirt sales.

Dystopia = Utopia + Time

Given enough time, any utopia imagined by a past generation always ends up sounding like a dystopian nightmare. Here's a summary of some classic utopian and dystopian societies. Try to guess from the descriptions if they were supposed to be utopian (U) or dystopian (D). Answers are at the bottom.

Title	Synopsis	Year
1. *The Republic*, by Plato	Society is fixed to a population of 5040. Women and children are considered property, owned by men.	380 BC
2. *Utopia*, by Thomas More	An island of six thousand households. No private property. Every home has slaves. There is a welfare state. The state can engage in euthanasia.	1516
3. *A Crystal Age*, by W.H. Hudson	Humans shun technology in favour of a simpler pastoral life in which the only machine they have is a goblet producing ambient music. Only the queen and the alpha male in each household are allowed to mate.	1887
4. *The Republic of the Future*, by Anna B. Dodd	Humans live in identical homes and men and women dress alike. People work only two hours per day, but travel is forbidden and mediocrity is strictly enforced by law. Anyone more gifted than average is exiled.	1887
5. *The Machine Stops*, by E.M. Forster	Humans live underground in separate cells where their every need is taken care of by a machine, which they worship as though it's a god.	1909
6. *Herland*, by Charlotte P. Gilman	Society consists only of women, who have lived without men for two thousand years and now reproduce asexually. Only the most virtuous women are allowed to procreate.	1915
7. *Brave New World*, by Aldous Huxley	In the year 2540, people take part in regular orgies under the influence of a special antidepressant that lets them learn in their sleep. The lower classes are engineered to be less intelligent/curious than the upper classes.	1932
8. *Logan's Run*, by William F. Nolan	Citizens live in a domed city in which you can indulge in as much sex and hedonism as they like, until their twenty-first birthday, when they're killed.	1976

TL;DR: The only difference between a utopia and a dystopia is how much time has passed. Which is both a compliment to humanity's progress and an insult to its imagination.

Answers: 1:U, 2:U, 3:U, 4:D, 5:U, 6:U, 7:D, 8:D

History According to Hegel: Putting the Pro in Process

A concept changing into its opposite isn't restricted to utopian ideas. The philosophical theory behind this phenomenon is called the dialectic method. It dates to the Ancient Greeks and refers to discourse occurring when people who have different ideas come together and, through discussion, reach an understanding, overcoming the original beliefs that divided them. Ideally, it works like this:

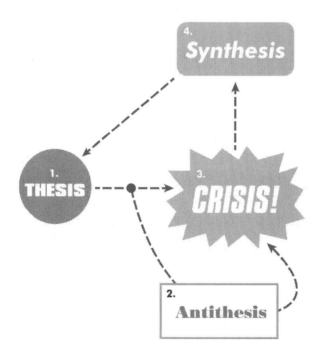

1. Thesis = the status quo, and so the starting point of the process (e.g. tyranny)

2. Antithesis = the opposite of the status quo (e.g. freedom)

3. Crisis = the clashing of the thesis and antithesis, which results in . . .

4. Synthesis = PROGRESS. The result of that clash. The resolution of those two ideas into a newer, richer idea (e.g. the constitution of laws—elements of freedom and tyranny combined into something workable, or at least profitably sue-able).

Although it's an ancient method, an eighteenth-century philosopher called Georg W.F. Hegel is most often associated with it. In his works, he tried to show that history proceeds in dialectic movements. How can history be dialectic? Well, each concept or thesis carries its antithesis within itself. For instance, while authority represents obedience, its opposite defines rebellion. In this way, authority already contains within itself its own antithesis. The crisis between obedience and rebellion can lead to a synthesis that overcomes authority: independence. Just think of the relationship dynamics between a child and his or her parents. From obedience to rebellion to an independent adult who needs neither to follow nor fight (but who might still occasionally call when he or she wants a handout).

For Hegel, history is the embodiment of the continuous cycle of different concepts clashing and synthesising into something better. Because of this, Hegel felt that history progresses. Each time we run around the thesis/antithesis/synthesis loop, a better concept emerges. This process will then end at, some point, with a perfect, absolute idea which contains no more contradictions to be overcome. There will be no more opposition to the status quo (who had some great early albums, after all), no more crises, no more synthesis. Consequently, history will end at this point; bad news for historians.

This idea was perhaps the greatest single influence on Karl Marx's work. Marx thought it was not abstract ideas that were at the foundation of this dialectical historical process but rather the constant battle of rulers vs. the ruled, the so-called class struggle. While both felt history would end, Hegel's perfect absolute idea was abstract, while for Marx, the finality would be socialism, which would remove all class struggle and therefore the need for a dialectic process. Socialism removed the need for much more than that, as it turned out (free will, autonomy, exotic holidays, etc. etc.), but it was nice of Marx to try. The dialectic process probably hasn't turned out quite as well as Hegel intended either, and across most of the world is probably closer to - 1. Thesis, 2. Antithesis, 3. Bar Brawl, 4. Hospital.

TL;DR: For Hegel, history itself is a dialectical process where each idea (thesis) contains within itself its opposite (antithesis). Society works through the clash of these two opposing ideas (crisis) to create a new idea (synthesis), which then becomes the next thesis to over-come. Humanity is still waiting eagerly for the synthesis that helps us overcome the crisis of having run out of weekend.

Posthumorous Legacy

It's long been said that death is the great equaliser. While that might be true, our legacies after we die are not equal. We lose control of them (and our bowels). Just as utopian ideas can become dystopian with the passing of time, so the public's perception of a person can also change. Some get lucky, with death high-fiving them posthumously, while others get posthumously legacy-slapped.

+	Before death	Legacy after
Confucius	Giant failure.	The gold standard for almost all societal questions in China for two thousand years.
Diogenes of Sinope	Lived in a barrel and masturbated in public.	Made fun of for living in barrel and masturbating in public but is also included in this table!
Vincent van Gogh	One-eared, insane painter. Only ever sold one picture while alive.	Beloved and influential one-eared, insane painter with his own museum and record-breaking sales.
Alan Turing	Convicted of "indecency" for being homosexual, which led to his suicide.	Acknowledgement that he almost single-handedly cracked the Enigma code and shortened World War II by years. National hero.
Princess Diana	Professional waver, ribbon cutter, hat wearer.	Global martyr. The people's princess.

-	Before death	Legacy after
Friedrich Nietzsche	All-round smart guy emancipating humankind.	Giant Nazi (thanks, sis!). More on this in Seating 80.
Karl Marx	Fought for equality and human betterment.	Ideas used to justify mass murder. "The death of one man is a tragedy; the death of millions is a statistic," said Stalin.
Che Guevara	Anti-capitalist.	Face became capitalism's go-to revolutionist clip art.
Josef Stalin	Considered a fairly benign dictator by many.	Unmasked (fairly) as one of his century's worst dictators/most prolific killers.

TL;DR: After you die you lose control over what people think of you. But since you're dead, it doesn't really matter anyway. If you don't want people to find the skeletons in your closet, it's probably better to bury them in the yard.

CHAPTER 10

NIHILISM AND WORSHIP

NIHILISM:
For people with nothing in common.

The Smugness of Grocery Picking

Imagine you're back in a supermarket. As you walk the aisles, you do your best to avoid unhealthy temptations such as sugar-glazed doughnuts, intoxicating alcohol, and delicious, fatty cheeses. Proud of your prudence, you finally make it to the cashier and tip out your modest basket: lettuce (grown locally); tomatoes (organic); avocado (fair trade); bread (whole grain); yogurt (from happy cows); and lastly, as a little treat to yourself, a can of Coke Zero. You look down and feel proud of your self-restraint. You're showing everyone what a paragon of noble shopping and self-restraint you really are.

Then, behind you, a scruffy-looking guy arrives in a leather jacket and begins unpacking his basket onto the conveyor belt. You look down at it: potato chips (the cheap ones); five beers (the strongest ones); M&M's (XXL family size); and lastly, as a little treat to himself, a two-litre bottle of Jägermeister. "Excuse me," he says, and leans past you to the push the button for cigarettes. *F-i-v-e times.*

How do you think you would feel in this moment? Probably quite smug, right?

Because of your healthy choices, you'll probably live much longer than he will, chewing on organic lettuce leaves. But cavemen only ate organic too, didn't they? There wasn't anything else. And hunting mammoths and running from sabre-tooth cats was certainly a better workout than the irregular, half-hearted cardio you do (or rather, always intend to do) at the gym. There was also no pollution, and no one had invented the nine-to-five work week. And yet, our distant ancestors rarely lived past thirty!

And while the man in the leather jacket, with the questionable groceries, might die younger and with fewer teeth, he's probably going to have a hell of a lot more fun living. Let's face it, even lettuce would eat crisps and chocolate if it could.

By abstaining, how much time are we really buying for ourselves and at what point is it no longer worth it?

Perhaps, to borrow the words of author Hunter S. Thompson, "Life should not be a journey to the grave with the intention of arriving safely in a pretty and well-preserved body, but rather to skid in broadside in a cloud of smoke, thoroughly used up, totally worn out, and loudly proclaiming 'Wow! What a Ride!'"

We're all making the wager that our life will be long if we respect it and delay gratification. If you knew that next week, with certainty, you would be killed by a falling piano, would the contents of your supermarket basket be the same as they are today? We're all making bets on an unknown future—it's just that some of us are scoffing great mouthfuls of Ben and Jerry's Half Baked while doing so.

TL; DR: There are many ways in which we sacrifice in the present in the hope of rewards in an uncertain future. If you want to buy Jägermeister and fancy cheese today, do it. Tomorrow be damned.

Winning Big Winning Big with Pascal's Wager

In the seventeenth century, French mathematician and philosopher Blaise Pascal looked rationally and pragmatically at whether we should believe in God. His logic was as follows.

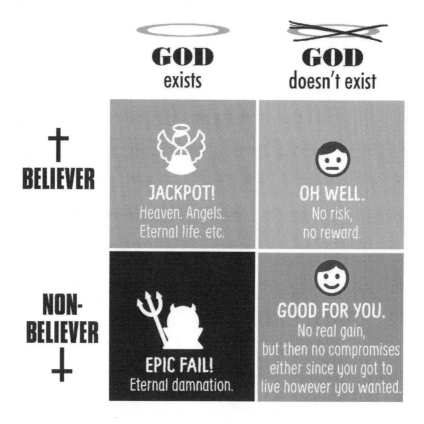

Pascal concluded that because the pros of believing are immeasurably larger than the cons of believing (not sinning, avoiding certain foods, attending boring religious services, and wearing silly hats), so suck it up and believe already, or, at least pretend to.

Does it make sense to cover your bets and just fake belief?

Today, in all our modern, enlightened wonder, we might laugh at the simplicity of Pascal's wager. Because even if an afterlife does exist, there are several obvious flaws in his hack.

A) "Fake it 'til you make it." God is smart enough to have created life, including you, and vengeful enough to be able to banish you to eternal hellfire, yet not observant enough to notice you trying to trick him? *Hmm.* Pascal was aware of this but felt that God would (like that time you tried to cook soufflé for your beloved and accidentally burnt down half the kitchen) appreciate the effort.

B) The one true God? Whether we call God Allah, Krishna, Flying Spaghetti Monster, or G'man might make no difference. In the end, they might all be one. But it's also possible that you wait your entire lifetime for one to show up only to die and have ten appear. Will you have picked the right one to worship?

C) You can't just believe something you don't believe in. Pascal's "fake it 'til you make it" is a nice idea but hard in practice. Belief works like chores: the more you tell yourself you have to do them, the more you resent the effort and obligation. That's not much of a basis on which to develop real, genuine faith.

D) Does God even care? Most of the major religions depict God as a heavily bearded, omnipotent, finicky nightclub bouncer who will send you away for even the slightest flaw in your moral dress code. But what if big old G couldn't care less if you worship him or not? What evidence is there that he does? If we had that evidence, well, we wouldn't need Pascal's wager now, would we?

E) Are the costs of believing really that little? Depending which hell-avoidance club you join, you might lose bacon sandwiches, premarital sex, or opening the fridge on the Sabbath. Even if you succeed in believing (and nice job on that), you've altered who you are. You're a different person, perhaps one less inclined to work on something to solve the mysteries of the here and now.

TL; DR: The philosopher and mathematician Blaise Pascal

famously made a wager involving finite earthly gratification and infinite eternal damnation. He concluded that it's better to believe in God and be wrong than to not believe in God and spend an afterlife in hell. Even if it means spending this life wearing silly hats and getting up early on Sundays.

Arguments for the Existence of Unicorns

There are arguments for the existence of a supreme deity. However, most could "prove" equally improbable things like unicorns.

Arguments	God	Unicorns
Ontological argument	1. God is the greatest conceivable being. 2. It is greater to exist than not to exist. 3. Therefore, God must exist.	1. Unicorns are the greatest conceivable animals. 2. It is greater to exist than not to exist. 3. Therefore, unicorns must exist.
Creationist argument	Life is so complex it must have been designed by some intelligent being.	If that being was intelligent enough to have designed something as complex as all of life, would it be stupid enough to leave out unicorns? *No.*
Biblical argument	Certain aspects of the Bible have proved to be true. Since the Bible makes no sense without God's existence, God exists.	Unicorns are mentioned multiple times in the Bible; e.g. Isaiah 34:7 "And the unicorns shall come down with them." Therefore, unicorns exist.
Testimonial argument	I know that God exists because I can feel his presence.	I know that unicorns exist because I have seen them on TV multiple times.
Contrarian argument	You can't prove God *doesn't* exist.	You can't prove unicorns *don't* exist.
Coercive argument	If you don't believe in God, you'll go to hell.	If you don't believe in unicorns, you'll go to unicorn hell*.

*Equally hot but with more rainbows and strawberry sprinkles.

Fact File: Friedrich Nietzsche

· F. Nietzsche ·

Influence: 7/10

Nationality: German

Dates: 1844 – 1890

Groupies: His sister, who was married to a prominent Nazi. After Nietzsche's death, she completely misinterpreted his work, even falsified certain passages, to cater to her and her husband's own fascist propaganda.

Bio: Nietzsche is often referred to as "the great destroyer"; someone who believed philosophy should be taught with a hammer, not a quill. A hammer that he encouraged humanity to swing at all its idols. For him, worship, and the idea that something is above us and better than us, was an abomination. He believed it's precisely the reverse that sets us free: accepting that nothing is above us and that we must worship no one, thing, or idea.

Greatest Idea: Transvaluation of values, aka "God is dead. (God remains dead. And we have killed him)". Nietzsche believed in destroying truths to reveal the conventions and traditions sheltering behind them. The truth about truths, he believed, is that they are necessary lies we keep telling ourselves to feel better about and legitimise the world and its (often unfair) social structures. What would be left after we get rid of religion, science, and all the other structures of meaning? How could we live without false idols? For Nietzsche, this world wouldn't be scary but beautiful, the ultimate affirmation of life, one in which we are free to embrace our role as the only creators of our meaning.

Worst Idea: Outsmarting his audience. Today he is widely regarded as one of philosophy's biggest misogynists: "You're going to (visit) women? Don't forget the whip!" However, he said this in reference to Mary Wollstonecraft, a women's rights activist who argued that everyone is born with equal rights but that society takes them away, leaving women without education as little more than cattle. Therefore, she said, the appropriate wedding gift for a groom is a horsewhip. In referencing this great philosopher, who never got the attention she undoubtedly deserved, Nietzsche accidentally cemented his reputation as a misogynist.

Anecdote: While still in school, Nietzsche was caught drunk with a friend. He was so ashamed of the incident that he wrote his mother a long, heart-wrenching letter saying he would understand if she never wanted to speak to him again and that alcohol reverts us to levels of culture that we've already overcome. Later he realised the error in his ways and argued the opposite: "For art to exist, for any sort of aesthetic activity to exist, a certain physiological precondition is indispensable: intoxication." So, the next time you're drunk, just tell your peers that you're doing creative work and that there's profound nobility in your heroic devotion to the cause! *Burp*. Cheers!

Quotes:

"Without music, life would be a mistake." *Easy to say when you live in a time without Nickelback or Justin Bieber.*

"That which does not kill us makes us stronger." *He seemed to forget about trauma and brain damage.*

"In individuals, insanity is rare; but in groups, parties, nations and epochs, it is the rule." *Obvious to anyone who's ever attended a bachelor party.*

Nietzsche in Objects:

1. God is dead sticker: His most famous phrase.

2. Richard Wagner dartboard: Wagner was first his friend then later a mortal enemy.

3. My little pony: He hugged a pony being beaten right before he had a complete mental breakdown.

4. Medicine: He was a sickly man who suffered heavy migraines and was constantly ill (probably related to the syphilis he contracted).

5. Academic regalia: He was a philological genius (fluent in Ancient Greek and Latin) and was appointed professor of philology at the

age of twenty-four. However, his academic work was never appreciated during his lifetime.

6. Beaker: At one point he became determined to drop philosophy and study chemistry instead. "That which does not kill us makes us stronger" would have turned into "What doesn't react will have to be heated longer".

7. Pop-culture equivalent: Thor. Nietzsche is known as the big destroyer, someone who famously said that philosophy is best done with a hammer. Unlike the Norse god, Nietzsche was of frail posture and not much of a physical threat. But if aggravated, he could release his army of Übermenschen (more on those in Seating 84) and have them smash happily away at society's traditions and beliefs.

TL;DR: Nietzsche was a moustachioed German philosopher who believed life has no meaning and that accepting this, and creating our own meaning anyway, is both beautiful and gets us closer to becoming an Übermensch (not the German word for a cab driver).

The Rise and Fall (and Rise) of Meaningless Man

Unassociated Press, 1.2.15

Austin, Texas:

"SUPERHERO" ATTACKS CHURCH.

Worshippers in Austin were stunned today when a church service was interrupted by a "superhero". This interloper, dressed in brown spandex with a giant red cross on his chest, forcefully knocked a priest from his podium before delivering his own special sermon. "I cannot believe in a god who wants to be praised all the time," he said. "Is man merely a mistake of God's? Or is God merely a mistake of man? I would believe only in a god that knows how to dance," he said, before breaking into a somewhat sloppy rendition of the Macarena.

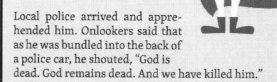

Local police arrived and apprehended him. Onlookers said that as he was bundled into the back of a police car, he shouted, "God is dead. God remains dead. And we have killed him."

"If anything killed God, it was probably this man's dancing," said churchgoer Melanie Roberts. "Well, that and Judas."

15.2.15

VANITY UNFAIR

VIRAL SENSATION MEANINGLESS MAN STRIKES AGAIN.

Internet viral sensation Meaningless Man has racked up more than five million views in just three days on a flashmob video filmed at a Miss World pageant. Meaningless Man and hundreds of his followers, carrying anti-Miss World banners with slogans such as, "What do we want? Nothing. When do we want it? Repeatedly", and "There are no beautiful surfaces without a terrible depth", flooded the stage, dancing their trademark Macarena, in silence, as security fought to remove them. "And those who were seen dancing were thought to be insane by those who could not hear the music," said Meaningless Man, as he was bundled away once again.

NEW JOKE TIMES

4. 8. 2015

Meaningless Man speaks!

Internet phenomenon and so-called anti-icon Meaningless Man has released his first public statement, and it's to announce his retirement. "I cannot continue," the caped crusader told his fans. "For while I am pleased that you are listening to my message, that life is meaningless and that's okay, through my success I have become the thing I hate. I wanted only to teach you about the danger of idols, and in doing so I have become an idol. I have thought long and hard about what to do next. I cannot kill myself, for then I might become a martyr. I cannot continue because I only obfuscate my true message. Which is nothing. So, I'm retiring." "The author must keep his mouth shut when his work starts to speak."

DAILY PLANETS, 21. 4. 2072:

Meaningless Man's posthumous galactic takeover. Fifty years ago today, a strange, mustachioed earth anti-hero called Meaningless Man spread across Internet 1.0. Since then, his following has grown slowly, from non-believer to non-believer, and today, decades after his death, 64 percent of Milky Way residents identify as members of his Non-Church of the Much Latter in the Day Non-Saints of Meaninglessness. "First the day after tomorrow must come for me. Some men are born posthumously," he once said, and time has proven him correct.

TL;DR: If Marvel had existed in Nietzsche's time, the philosopher would have petitioned them to create a new superhero called Meaningless Man, who would preach a doctrine of nothingness and anti-worship.

This Is . . . Worship

A recent study concluded that China is the most godless place on earth, where only 7 percent of people feel religious. But what if the other 93 percent of people are just kidding themselves? Can there be such a thing as atheism?

In 2005, author David Foster Wallace gave a famous commencement speech entitled "This Is Water". It began with the following story: Two young fish are swimming along when they happen to meet an older fish swimming the other way. It nods at them, and says, "Morning, boys. How's the water?" The young fish swim on for a bit, and then eventually one of them looks over at the other and asks, "What the hell is water?"

It's incredibly hard to see and talk about the most obvious aspects of reality. This truism is almost a cliché. The more self-evident something is, the more likely we are to forget about it.

Wallace believed there is no such thing as *not* worshipping. This doesn't mean we're all spiritual, but that we all must turn to something to provide us with meaning. We all cherish something and, by virtue of it, worship. Wallace considered this a fact, and not necessarily a problem if we carefully choose what to worship. The bigger problem is unawareness—not choosing for ourselves and so letting society choose for us. It is critically important, therefore, to choose wisely and continuously re-evaluate because otherwise, "pretty much anything else you worship will eat you alive".

"If you worship money and things . . . then you will never feel you have enough . . . Worship your body and beauty and sexual allure and you will always feel ugly . . . Worship power, you will end up feeling weak and afraid, and you will need ever more power over others to numb you to your own fear . . . Worship your intellect, being seen as smart, you will end up feeling stupid, a fraud, always on the verge of being found out."

Wallace felt that it's through worship that you to see what it is that you really care about. But unmanaged, unacknowledged worship will be your downfall. It is not the worship that we openly declare that we should be fearful of, but the worship that we slip into gradually. Because unaware of your idols, you're as blind as the fish that can't recognise water while swimming in it.

TL;DR: Even if Nietzsche is right and God is dead, worship certainly isn't. The real value of education and awareness is that they prevent you from slipping into an unaware state of it. If that fails, this awareness is also great at helping you come up with good post-hoc rationalisations should you decide to cannonball into worship's deep end.

Just Worship It Already

Humans are very creative when it comes to veneration and reverence. We can convince ourselves that almost anything is worthy of worship, including reality-show-casted boy bands. Here's a rundown of some of humanity's strangest idols.

1. The Flying Spaghetti Monster

Believers of this parody religion call themselves Pastafarians. The movement began when a physics graduate sent a letter to the Kansas State Board of Education protesting the teaching of creationism. Since there's no scientific merit in creationism, he also wanted his made-up deity, the Flying Spaghetti Monster, to be recognised and taught. Since then it has become an Internet sensation with a faithful following.

2. Prince Philip

Even legendary royal buffoon and political incorrectness personified is worshipped as a god on a small island in Vanuatu. Locals there had a legend that foretold of an earth spirit who travelled far away and married a powerful woman. When Queen Elizabeth visited the island in 1974, with Prince Philip in tow, the followers of the movement decided he had to be this long-lost earth spirit.

3. French racing driver Claude Vorilhon, aka. Raël

Followers of Raëlism believe that Claude was abducted by aliens and travelled to a distant planet called Elohim, where he met the who's who of other deities and learnt that humanity was created by alien DNA some twenty-five-thousand years ago. Oh, and the aliens are coming back. They'll be stopping by Jerusalem in 2025. Best reserve your hotel room early.

4. Gadget Hackwrench from Disney's *Chip 'n' Dale: Rescue Rangers*

There's a small Russian cult that worships a fictional mouse from this TV show from the nineties. Gadget Hackwrench is an inventor and mechanic, a kind of MacGyver for kids. Or, as one of her worshippers put it, "The most untouched and perfect sibling of the great God on Earth." *Okay* . . .

5. Chhinnamasta

A beheaded Hindu and Buddhist goddess of self-sacrifice and sexual restraint. After she and her followers bathed for too long, which led to extreme hunger, she beheaded herself to allow them to drink her blood. She was obviously not a big believer in sandwiches.

6. Baron Samedi

If you like your gods with a side order of rock 'n' roll, Baron Samedi is your man. A Haitian voodoo god, the good Baron is a skeleton wearing a tuxedo, top hat, and sunglasses who welcomes you in the afterlife and leads you to the underworld all while swearing profusely, smoking a cigar, and drinking rum.

TL;DR: You can worship pretty much anything if you put your mind to it, or, better, don't!

Amor Fati, or How I Learnt to Stop Worrying and Love the Übermensch

Few concepts in philosophy are as famous—and as completely misunderstood—as Nietzsche's Übermensch. As badass as the word sounds, it has nothing to do with fascism, tall blond people, or on-demand taxi services. Instead, at its core, it's about the death of God. But not *that* God, the bearded omnipotent guy on the fluffy cloud. To Nietzsche, "God" was more of a broad concept that stood for any idea or dogma that promotes forsaking something in this world in favour of getting something in the next (e.g. getting into heaven if you successfully stick to the rules of your church).

Nietzsche believed that dogmas belittle the one life we have. If you're convinced of an afterlife where dozens of virgins wait patiently for you, in lingerie, while an angel hovers, harp in hand, to serenade you, what incentive do you have to really live *here*? Or to help improve society? Why not just end your life prematurely?

But then, at the same time, if we give up the comfortable fallacies that give our lives meaning, are we not left with only a meaningless existential void?

Yes. Exactly. That's the point.

For Nietzsche, this meaninglessness is not a bug—it's a feature. Rather than being slaves to someone else's prescribed meaning, we should take the first positive step towards creating meaning for ourselves, towards becoming an Übermensch, and abandon our gods. Rather than slipping into nihilism, the Übermensch simply acknowledges his or her role as the only creator of his or her own meaning. Life is utterly meaningless (that's a given), but deciding, nevertheless, to create your meaning is THE ULTIMATE AFFIRMATION OF LIFE ITSELF!

Do it and you'll fall in love with your fate (*amor fati*: "love of fate", in Latin). Here's how Nietzsche put it:

"My formula for greatness in a human being is amor fati: *that one wants nothing to be different, not forward, not backward, not in all eternity. Not merely bear what is necessary, still less conceal it—all idealism is mendacity in the face of what is necessary—but love it."*

If you find that a bit hard going, he also allegedly said, "You have your way. I have my way. As for the right way, the correct way, and the only way, it does not exist." So go create your own way and don't be trapped by slave morality, my dear Übermensch.

TL;DR: If you choose to, you can look upon the meaninglessness of your existence, accept it, and build a life full of your own meaning. Do so and you transform into an Übermensch. If that sounds too difficult, you can also quit and be touched by the sacred, noodly appendages of the one true god: the Flying Spaghetti Monster.

CHAPTER 11

WORDS AND LANGUAGE

Cowboy vs. Indian: A Wordless Encounter

Imagine a wide open prairie, the air shimmering in the heat. A cowboy is riding his trusty steed home when he meets an Indian heading in the opposite direction. They circle each other on their horses, skeptically, until the Indian breaks the tension by raising his hand and pointing slowly at the cowboy. The cowboy is taken aback but shows no fear. In turn, he makes the victory sign with two fingers. This perplexes the Indian, and he responds by angling both arms over his head so that his hands touch at the top, forming a triangle. At this point the cowboy cracks a smile, relaxes into his saddle, and raises his hand to his chest. He then moves his open palm forward in a wiggling motion, like a slithering snake. After a few tense moments, the two pass each other disappearing into the scenery, the Indian with a puzzled look, the cowboy cocksure.

That night at home, the cowboy recounts what happened to his beloved wife: "I always knew that the Indians were cowards," he says. "Picture this! On my way home, an Indian jumps me and threatens to shoot me, point-blank." He repeats the gesture, pointing at his wife. "But I stood my ground and made clear to him that I would shoot him twice before he could even pull once." He makes the victory sign. "Anyway, so the coward backs down and tells me he just wants to go back to his tent." Again, he mimics the Indian, making the triangular sign. "But as you know I'm a good man, so I told him I'd let him and his empty threat slip this time if he slid off home," he says, showing the meandering snake motion. "I sure showed him." The cowboy spits into the dirt.

Upon the Indian's arrival home, he too regales his wife with the story: "Darling, you wouldn't believe the strange thing that happened to me. I met another crazy white man. I'm on the prairie and I see this cowboy, so I ask him who he is, gesturing at him with my index finger. And what does he answer? He tells me that he's a goat! So I figure he's spent too much time in the sun, but I play along and I ask him if he's a mountain goat." He shows his wife the triangular sign. "He responds, 'No, I'm a river goat.'" He makes the serpentine movement with his arm. "Idiot." He shakes his head.

While it's clear that the cowboy and the Indian had a conversation, it's also clear that they didn't manage to exchange meaning, given the lack of a common language. But is it ever clear what somebody wants to say, even if all participants do speak the same language? Could it be that most philosophical problems arise from "conversations" like this one on the prairie? The philosopher most famous for investigating this problem is Ludwig Wittgenstein.

TL;DR: While we might be able to control what we want to say, we have no idea what the other person will understand. River goats are a philosophically endangered species.

Fact File: Ludwig Wittgenstein

Influence: 7/10

Nationality: Austrian

Facts: 1889 – 1951

Groupies: All twentieth-century philosophers had something to say about him, if
only to say that they didn't like him.

Bio: Ludwig Wittgenstein believed that all
problems of philosophy are, in essence,
problems of misguided language. For him,
it's misunderstanding the logic of our
languages that leads us to ask questions that
seem legitimate but are just meaningless
utterings, such as Noam Chomsky's famous phrase "Colourless
green ideas sleep furiously". There are no real misunderstandings,
or questions that can't be answered, when we form the questions
correctly.

Greatest Idea: "The limits of my language are the limits of my
mind. All I know is what I have words for." Wittgenstein felt sure
that language shapes reality and the world is fundamentally different
depending on the words or language you use to describe it. Meaning
is not an abstract thing but something enmeshed in social context.
The way we understand, interact with, and explain the world is

dependent upon the way the language in which we think and communicate works (usage, grammar, meaning, etc).

Worst Idea: Wittgenstein was born into the second-wealthiest family in Austria-Hungary (they had thirteen mansions in Vienna alone!). When his father died, Wittgenstein decided a humbler life-style would suit him better, and gave his wealth to his brothers and sisters, believing they were already corrupted by wealth anyway. He then took modesty too far and found himself destitute but was too proud to ask his friends or family for money. In the end, his sister rescued him when she decided to build yet another mansion (thirteen is just not enough, right?) and employed him as her architect.

Anecdote: Wittgenstein's PhD defence at Cambridge allegedly ended with him clapping his two examiners on the shoulders and saying, "Don't worry, I know you'll never understand it." The two examiners were Bertrand Russell and G. E. Moore, two of the most famous twentieth-century philosophers. Moore's report stated: "In my opinion this is a work of genius; it is, in any case, up to the standards of a degree from Cambridge."

Quotes:

"If people never did silly things nothing intelligent would ever get done." *That at least explains tattoos, war, and deep-fried Mars bar.*

"The riddle does not exist. If a question can be put, then it can also be answered." *Which doesn't mean you'll like the answer or remember where you put it.*

"A man will be imprisoned in a room with a door that's unlocked and opens inwards; as long as it does not occur to him to pull rather than push." *If he's bamboozled by that door, it's probably safest he stays in there, since he's really going to struggle with feeding himself, fathers-in-law, and quantitative easing.*

Wittgenstein in Objects:

1. Patent: He studied engineering in Manchester, where he worked on plane engines and even received a patent for one of his works.

2. Fire poker: Allegedly he used a poker to intimidate another philosopher during a particularly heated debate.

3. Norbert Davis detective novel: Wittgenstein adored these.

4. Rainbow: He was homosexual but never admitted this since it was illegal at the time.

5. Austrian fin-de-siècle art: He was born and raised in Austria, and heir to a very wealthy family.

6. Gramophone: Music was important to him, and he could whistle entire symphonies from memory.

7. Fly in a bottle: Wittgenstein coined the famous phrase "To show the fly the way out of the fly-bottle."

Pop-culture equivalent: Count von Count from *Sesame Street*. Both grew up in a castle. Much like the count tries to educate children on simple mathematical concepts, Wittgenstein wrote most of his texts in an approachable format. While he didn't laugh maniacally like the count, he did have a good sense of humour and once quipped that you could write an entire philosophy book just in jokes (we're doing our best to prove that). Last but not least, both were noble in their appearance, even hinting at vanity.

TL;DR: Ludwig Wittgenstein was an Austrian philosopher who believed that all problems of philosophy are, in essence, problems of language: "Philosophy is a battle against the bewitchment of our intelligence by means of language." *Nice try, fancy witch-phrase! Let's burn it.*

Indirect Language: the Direct Way to Better Understanding

If language is the main window to communication, why do we smear it up with unclear phrasing, indirect wording, idioms, and innuendo?

What we say	What we mean
Let's agree to disagree.	You're wrong, but I'm tired.
It would be nice if you would visit your grandma.	Not only should you visit your dear old neglected grandma, you should *want* to visit her.
Would you like to pick me up from the airport tomorrow?	I know you wouldn't like to pick me up from the airport, but I need a lift and this relationship is important to you, right?
I guess you *could* do it that way, yes.	I guess you could do it that way, yes, if you were an idiot.
I just have a few short comments.	I'm easing you in gently, but you might as well empty your calendar—this is going to be rough. And will take all night.
Nice face you've got there. Would be a real shame if something happened to it.	Do as I say or I will punch you. In the face.
Would you like to come back to mine for a drink?	Would you like to come back to mine and have sex with me? We could probably also have a drink first, if you insist.

Why don't we all just say exactly what we mean? Why do we need indirect language? Well, there are very good reasons.

Plausible deniability. If you're not sure if both parties are on the same page about what's really being discussed, indirect language can prevent awkwardness and confrontation. "A cooperative listener can accept the request, but an uncooperative one cannot react adversarially to it," says writer Steven Pinker, a pioneer of the topic, in a landmark paper entitled "The Logic of Indirect Speech." If you get pulled over for speeding, asking the officer "Will you accept a bribe to make this go away?" gets you in big trouble if the answer is no. Slipping fifty dollars on top of your driver's licence implies this but leaves you both an out: "I'm sorry, officer, I've no idea how that fifty-dollar note got there. *A bribe? Well, of course not.*"

Relationship negotiation. Language is not only used to convey meaning but also to negotiate the types of relationship people have with each other. Consider the following relationship types.

Dominant: "Don't mess with me" gets expressed as "It's a lovely day for you to go outside for a walk while you've still got two legs."

Communal: "Share and share alike" gets expressed as "It's a lovely day for likeminded friends to be out for a walk, isn't it?"

Reciprocal: The good old "tit for tat" gets expressed as "It's a lovely day for you to walk to the shop and buy sweets for us while I stay in and do the washing up."

Indirect language allows its users to cover themselves, implying that a certain relationship type exists under the surface of the words spoken. Therefore, Pinker says, in the same paper, it "should be judged as generating less awkwardness and discomfort, as being more respectful, as better acknowledging the expected relationship with the hearer (such as affection, deference, or collegiality), and as making it easier for the participants to resume their normal relationship should the offer be rebuffed." And if it doesn't work there's always running away, blocking each other on social media, and getting a restraining order.

TL;DR: You're more likely to get what you want if you don't ask directly. Unless you're better armed than the other party, in which case innuendo is totally optional.

The Own-Car Effect

It's perhaps logical that the Inuit people have more words to describe snow than the Bedouins, who roam Africa's deserts. Similarly, Hawaiians have 108 names for sweet potato, and the Baniwa tribe an impressive twenty-nine for ants (which perhaps implies they've very few words for insect repellent). But beyond linguistic dexterity and showing off during snowstorms/sandstorms, does it make a difference?

Do you think your experiences and tastes would be any different if you had vastly more words to describe them?

Luckily, this question has been studied with indigenous tribes all over the world. One especially interesting tribe is the Himba, a nomadic tribe living mostly in the north of Namibia. Himba are very modest people—so modest that they have just four colour words: *zuzu* (dark blues, reds, greens, and purples), *vapa* (whites and yellows), *buru* (some shades of greens and blues) and *dambu* (other shades of greens, reds, and browns). Researchers sat them down to test whether it takes them more time than it takes an American to distinguish two colours (such as dark blue and purple) for which they have only one word, and whether Americans are faster at discriminating between shades of green (e.g. *buru* and *dambu*) for which most of us have just one word.

It turns out the answer is yes. Having fewer colour words does make you worse at distinguishing subtle differences in shades of them.

Although, under no circumstances, does anyone need fifty shades of grey.

Research with the Himba and similar tribes does show that people perceive the world differently based on language spoken and size of vocabulary. However, the size and quality of the difference is still an open question. It's not that we can't see a colour until we have a word for it; what's happening is probably more like the so-called own-car effect: buy a new car and suddenly the entire city seems to be filled with people driving the same one. Once you learn something exists, you start spotting it everywhere. You've probably experienced something similar with shoes, trees, authors, and songs.

In reality (unless you're starring in your own bizarre version of *The Truman Show*), these things were always there—they just weren't relevant to you before. Knowing a word for something helps you separate it from the heap of sensory stimuli constantly flooding your brain and demanding your attention. Our vocabularies, languages, cultures, hobbies, and interests all bias certain types of stimuli. They run ahead and highlight them for us, making them easier to spot.

TL;DR: If something is important to you, learn more words to describe its nuances. Our perception of reality does change based on the language we have to label it. This is exactly why you need 613 adjectives to describe chocolate cake.

New Words for Old Problems

If the limits of our language constitute the limits of our world and we want to build a snug little annex out the back of that world, all we need are some new words. An easy task, since life is full of phenomena that deserve to be labelled yet have no name and so are completely unplayable in Scrabble. To change that, and help you spot them in future, here are six neologisms.

1. Reprain: When someone expresses an utterly stupid opinion but social conventions prohibit you from laughing out loud or slapping them in the face. So, you just bite down on your lip, nod, and refrain from ridiculing them. "I was in hard reprain when Uncle Jimmy said we shouldn't drink tap water because the government puts chemicals in it to make us stupid."

2. Converlonesome: A situation where you try to break into a group at a party but their conversation never ends and no one makes space for you to join, so you just hover, unwelcome, like a priest at a school disco.

3. SURFACE-SAGE

3. Surface sage: A person who's able to pass themselves off as intelligent because of their appearance. "What he says is stupid, but he has a really long beard, wears glasses, and uses a pocket protector, so there must be something to it."

4. Cul-de-word-sac: Where you get so busy elaborating on an answer you forget what the question was. Unsure what to do so, you keep talking and talking and . . . "look, another squirrel!"

5. Soliphipster: A person with an uncanny talent for turning the conversation back to their field of expertise, no matter how tenuous the link. "Your ordering of the avocado salad reminds me of Pearl Jam's seminal 2006 album *Pearl Jam*, the second to feature producer Adam Kasper, an album which was, I feel, unfairly panned by the critics for being generic. Its album cover featured an avocado."

6. Politician: Someone with the cunning ability to answer a question in a way that leaves its asker more confused, and who then excessively taxes the asker for the privilege.

TL;DR: By not being bothered to read this page, you've missed out on awesome new words. Shame on you. If you did read the page and are still reading this TL;DR, nice one, legal eye (a person who always reads the small print).

Gettin' Dizzy in Hermeneutic Circles

Whether we're aware of it or not, we're constantly interpreting the world: is the man holding the door open for us because he wants to be nice or because he wants to inappropriately fondle us? "Hermeneutics" comes from the Greek word for "interpretation", and the hermeneutic circle is the process that happens when we extract meaning from texts.

The hermeneutic circle shows that to understand the whole of a text, you have to understand the parts. However, to understand the parts, you must also understand the whole. It's a (non-vicious) circle. For example, if you want to know what the whole of a book is all about, you begin with the individual sentences. From there you form opinions about its genre, style, and, from the language used, even its intended audience.

However, your understanding of each individual sentence is affected by your interpretation of the whole. For example, if the book describes nineteenth-century England, your knowledge of that time period increases as you read it, giving you better insight into what it was like to live back then, and more knowledge with which you can analyse the book's remaining individual sentences. As the expression goes, if you only have a hammer, everything starts to look like a nail. Going through the hermeneutic circle in various levels of interpretation arms you with wider, richer tools of comprehension.

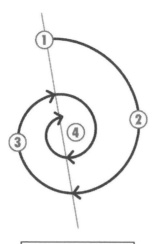

① First grasp
② Inspection of detail
③ Global inspection
④ Deeper understanding

Understanding is not a clear-cut process; there can be more than one meaning to a text, and each sentence reflects differently, depending on the light you shine upon it. Take George Orwell's book *Animal Farm*. Sentence by sentence, you can read it as a fable about animals bravely standing up for their rights. Or, depending on your knowledge of twentieth-century politics, you can read it as an allegory of the Russian Revolution.

You, the reader, are an active, essential part of the process. There is no interpretation independent of an interpreter. There is no finality, no eureka moment where the text's unique, true meaning is revealed. Instead, it's just you, moving in circles of understanding, adding your own interpretation, one loop at a time, trying not to get woozy on your way to wisdom.

TL;DR: We interpret what we read in hermeneutic circles. Interpret correctly and we get understanding; interpret incorrectly and we get a dead end, which we often interpret as some long, bricked-up tunnel to greater meaning.

There Is Something Fishy about Exegesis

While often used as a synonym for hermeneutics, "exegesis" is actually a fancy word for a mundane activity: interpreting theological texts. You'll see it in almost any church service, which usually begins with a priest quoting from the Bible. Perhaps something such as, "The lips of the wise spread knowledge; not so the hearts of fools" (Proverbs 15:7). He will then interpret this quote via our old friend exegesis to show how it really means that mobile phones reduce our attention spans and distract us from God, social media is all pointless vanity, and online dating undermines the sanctity of marriage.

Exegesis is a valuable tool for any *Fast* Philosopher, for it allows you to create ~~fictitious~~ meaning to back up your arguments and opinions. Let's look upon scripture from a more modern era, a prayer sung in the temples of today—discotheques. Really, it's a shame that these sweaty late-night techno sermons are generally regarded as banal or frivolous, for great minds are at work in them, such as Germany's H.P. Baxxter, better known as Scooter: a high priest of 160 bpm wisdom. Let us marvel now in the profundity of his teachings, drawing upon his seminal work.

How much is the fish?
Here we go, here we go
Here we go again
Yeeeeeeeeeah!
Sunshine in the air!
How much is the fish?
How much is the fish?
Yeah!
Come on, come on
Argh!
Resurrection!   – Scooter 19:98

Can it be mere coincidence that he talks of fish? Is it not more likely bordering on blatantly obvious that "fish" is an allegory for small groups of sincere believers? It is, after all, the same symbol that early-day Christians used to identify themselves. The "how much" asks the pertinent question of whether there's a price-tag for devoutness, and this leads to the deep spiritual insight that we can only receive if we are first willing to give. Next is "yeeeah!" We ask you, can there be anything more serene than the calming exclamation of utter joy expressed in "yeeeah"? No, there cannot.

Baxxter then continues transcending our expectations with his final "sunshine in the air!" Clearly, as we all know, sunshine is transported by massless photons and as such cannot be "in the air". So again, the meaning must lie deeper. It's obviously a promise of sincerity. A promise, if you will, that love will embrace all willing to let go, and float like air, in the warm sunshine of devotion! Of course!

That concludes this week's sermon. We're happy to leave our congregation blessed with strength and understanding. Next week we'll learn a tangible lesson about sensuality and rapture in "Na na na, come on, come on, come on I like it, like it". (Rihanna 20:11).

TL;DR: Exegesis is the art of interpreting (theological) texts. Often it means extracting so much meaning from a text that it leaves the text feeling both violated and in need of therapy.

Philosophy Bingo

Level	Kant	Greeks	-isms	Weird Words	Core Concepts
1	Categorical Imperative	Paradox	Hedonism	Virtue	Innate Ideas
2	Sapere Aude	Metaphysics	Monism / Dualism	Amor Fati	Ockham's Razor
3	A Priori / A Posteriori	Agnosticism	Determinism	Theodicy	Socratic Method
4	Synthetic Knowledge	Exegesis	Utilitarianism	Hermeneutics	Plato's Cave
5	Copernican Revolution	Syllogism	Nihilism	Phenomenology	Dialectical Arguments

(Title row: ★ PHILOSOPHY BINGO ★)

The Rules

- For every word you successfully use, you get a point. In order to pass the test, you must get at least twelve points.
- Every time you use a word incorrectly, are challenged on its meaning, or are asked to define it, you lose a point.
- As soon as you've used all the words in a category or row, award yourself a bonus point.

CHAPTER 12

SCIENCE AND PARADIGMS

Science Inc.
FIGHTING IGNORANCE
SINCE 1534.

Endless Tales of Infinite Monkeys

Since philosophy is better at questions than answers, for the last chapter, as a treat, we'll turn to science and maths. Unlike philosophy, maths should have definite answers for us, right? Even if we can't agree on the meaning of life, we can at least agree that 1 + 1 = 2, can't we? Here we will find certainty, and if that fails, at least we will find monkeys. And what's better than one monkey? Infinite monkeys. Here's our first brain-teaser.

If you had infinite monkeys, each of your monkeys had a typewriter, and you commanded them to type for infinity, would they produce the complete works of Shakespeare?

The argument against: they'd need to type 835,997 words in the right order, each word consisting of multiple characters, without a single mistake.

The argument for: infinity is a really, really long time. It's all the time, in fact.

What do you think? Decide now.

The answer is yes, they would. Because, *infinity*. Somewhere in the infinite output of those infinite monkeys would be the complete works of Shakespeare. We'd never find it, it would probably take a few squillion years, and we'd waste a lot of paper, but nevertheless, it would be there (a squillion is not a real unit of measure; don't use that around mathematicians—they will laugh at you).

If the answer to this brain-teaser is this obvious, why does it excite mathematicians? Two reasons. Firstly, again, *infinity*. It's such an alluring concept. Why do stuff like division and addition a bunch of times when you could do these things FOREVER! Secondly, it could mean that all answers are just a few monkeys away! Because wouldn't those tippy-tappy primates also produce all present and future scientific works? And art? All maths questions are provable either as true or false, aren't they? So surely the monkeys would solve them, too?

Ah-ha! *This* is why mathematicians find this teaser so ponder worthy. They want to know if they'd be out of a job or not.

Would infinite monkeys also solve every maths problem? Decide before you read the next seating.

TL;DR: Infinite monkeys on infinite typewriters would replicate the complete works of Shakespeare. Also, how do you motivate a monkey to type for infinity?

The Full Story about Gödel's Incompleteness Theorems

In the nineteenth century, mathematics came up with a bunch of very odd but useful concepts, such as non-Euclidean geometry, i.e. geometry in which parallel lines can meet (which later proved to be a building block for Einstein's theory of relativity). It suddenly seemed as if there was not one mathematics but a whole zoo of many, very weird mathematics.

Because of this, German mathematician Gottlob Frege made it his life's work to create an irrefutable, purely logical foundation for all of mathematics. It was called *Grundgesetze der Arithmetik* (*The Foundations of Arithmetic*), and he was just preparing to print the second copy of it when he got a letter from an English guy called Bertrand Russell, who pointed out a seemingly small mathematical problem he'd found that didn't fit within the *Grundgesetze*.

It's known as the barber paradox. It's a mathematical formulation less than a sentence long, but its consequences were so devastating to Frege that he abandoned his life's work. The paradox goes like this: think of a barber as a man who shaves all those, and those only, who do not shave themselves.

Got that? Right, next comes a simple-sounding question: does the barber shave himself?

See the problem? If he does, he violates the definition of being a barber; if he doesn't, the definition demands that he does. While it might sound mundane and overly contrived, for mathematicians it was a serious buzzcut, I mean, buzzkill.

Shit really hit the fan. Having realised that logic couldn't be the cornerstone upon which a proven version of mathematics was built, everyone involved in the endeavour became seriously worried, and thus this time period got the cool nickname "the Foundational Crisis of Mathematics". To solve it, David Hilbert, another German mathematician, proposed a new idea: even if maths has no irrefutable basis in logic, it should be possible be show that the axioms of mathematics are consistent and complete. A lot of people were happy with that. It became known as Hilbert's program, and with it, axioms became maths' rule book. Consistency means that these axioms don't contradict each other, and completeness demands that no rules are forgotten. If a system can be proven to be complete and consistent, it follows that all questions within this system would have a definitive answer.

So, in stark contrast to philosophy and art, mathematics could, after all, still rightfully claim that there was an answer to all its problems, and, thus, these problems could be solved by infinitely many monkeys (or, at least, computers).

Hilbert was still campaigning for his program when the next spoil-sport came along. Kurt Gödel, an Austrian logician, published his incompleteness theorems (I guess he just couldn't wait until he finished them. *Boom*). These theorems took a great dump on Hilbert's program, showing that there *will* always remain questions in mathematics which are neither provable nor refutable. *Balls.*

And so, we are where we are: no system of mathematics that says anything interesting can be both consistent and complete at the same time. Even worse, systems can't even prove their own consistency. If you had infinite monkeys/computers/time/paper/patience, you would be able to retype Shakespeare but you would never, sadly, be able to answer all the riddles of mathematics. There are, therefore, no irrefutable truths that differentiate the foundations of maths from any other game with rules (or from cricket—rules with a game). Most mathematicians are so ashamed of this that they mostly avoid talking about it—much like a person who stumbles over an inconvenient truth, picks himself up, and hurries away as if nothing has happened.

TL;DR: Philosophically speaking, there's not much of a difference between poetry and math. Having infinite monkeys is less fun than it sounds. No one is sure if the barber did or didn't shave himself but everyone's sure a single sentence can destroy a life's work, so it's best we stop here.

The Paradigm Shifts of Grandeur

Being human is having to regularly reconcile your delusions of grandeur with the discoveries of science and the popular wisdom of your day, one paradigm shift at a time. Here's a brief history of everything that we've lost (even though we never really had it to begin with).

What we used to believe	What we now know	Who we can blame?
The earth is the centre of the universe.	The sun is at the centre of our solar system, and the earth revolves around it.	Nicolaus Copernicus
Humans were created in God's own image.	Humans are apes + opposable thumbs.	Charles Darwin
We are in control of our own thoughts.	Childhood messes everyone up.	Sigmund Freud
We are the masters of our creations.	It's our creations that shape who we are.	Friedrich Kittler and Marshall McLuhan
We are benign and compassionate beings.	Given the "right" setting, i.e. in a place with people wearing white jackets, we will do pretty much anything.	Stanley Milgram
No machine could ever outsmart a human.	Humans get their arses handed to them by chess computers.	IBM's Deep Blue
You need to touch someone to have good sex with them.	Virtual experiences are better than real ones.	HD + tactile virtual reality*
Human consciousness is magical and unique.	Consciousness can easily be replicated inside a computer.	The singularity*
Humans are the smartest species in the galaxy.	Humans are the platypus of the galaxy.	First contact*
We can never travel faster than the speed of light. Time travel is impossible.	Future you is going to travel back in time and slap present you for your poor life choices.	Time travel*

TL;DR: You are great. Or at least you used to be great, but since we started this sentence, knowledge about humanity has progressed and now you're only considered kind of *meh*.

*Upcoming paradigm shifts. Stay tuned!

Fact File: Karl Popper

Influence: 5/10

Nationality: Austrian

Dates: 1902 – 1994

Groupies: Paul Feyerabend, Friedrich Hayek, George Soros

· K. Popper ·

Bio: Karl Popper was an Austro-British philosopher influential in social and political philosophy and widely respected as one of the greatest philosophers of science. In the words of mathematician Hermann Bondi, a friend of his, *"There is no more to science than its method, and there is no more to its method than Popper has said."*

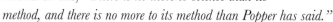

Greatest Idea: Falsifiability. Popper showed that the greatness of science lies not in proving hypotheses but in falsifying them, i.e. disproving them. Science uses induction: observations --> patterns --> hypotheses --> tests. Principles acquired through induction can never be proven—they can only be disproven. If you declare that all swans must be white, it takes only one black swan to prove that your "law of swans" was wrong. No matter how many white swans you observe, you'll never be sure that there isn't a black swan out there somewhere. Science doesn't provide truths, only hypotheses, and anything scientific, therefore, must be able to be proven incorrect. If something cannot be proven wrong under any account, it is merely myth, doctrine, or religion. In other words, a good theory distinguishes itself by making clear under which circumstances it falls apart.

Worst Idea: Read the footnotes! Popper was notoriously bad-tempered in the face of criticism, only willing to entertain it if the person could demonstrate full engagement and comprehension of his texts, including all footnotes. While Popper was teaching at the London School of Economics, the dean wanted to introduce a speed-reading course. The thought horrified Popper so much that he asked the dean to introduce a slow-reading course instead.

Anecdote: As a young man, Popper was a Marxist and a member of the Communist Party of Austria. In 1919, after eight of his friends were shot by police at a riot instigated by the party, Popper complained to its leaders about the outcome of their actions. He was told matter-of-factly that loss of life was inevitable in the run-up to a revolution. Popper disagreed, denounced Marxism, and remained committed to political tolerance and liberalism his entire life.

Quotes:

"Those who promise us paradise on earth never produced anything but a hell." *But those who promise us hell on earth are usually pretty good at keeping their word.*

"A theory that explains everything, explains nothing." *While a theory that explains nothing is best reserved for astrologists.*

"No rational argument will have a rational effect on a man who does not want to adopt a rational attitude." *Yeah, like, whatever!*

Popper in Objects:

1. Karl Marx dartboard: Popper denounced Marxism.

2. Poker: He was allegedly threatened with one by Wittgenstein.

3. Mouse door: He was a big believer in the open society.

4. Books: He learnt to be a bibliophile from his father, who had more than ten thousand books in his library.

5. Cabinet: He apprenticed as a cabinetmaker.

6. Certificate: He got his doctorate in psychology.

7. NZ flag: To avoid the war, he took a teaching job in New Zealand, where he lived for nine years; here, he wrote *The Open Society and Its Enemies*.

8. Pop-culture equivalent: Papa Smurf. Both were highly respected leaders of their tribe, wise, peaceful, energetic, and intellectually active well into their old age. Popper was still writing until weeks before his death at the age of 92 (Papa Smurf is 542, in case you're wondering. He doesn't look a day older than 535). Both lived in lush, green, slightly boring utopias (Smurfland and New Zealand). Papa Smurf fought Gargamel; Popper's enemy was political violence and bad science.

TL;DR: Austrian philosopher Karl Popper is famous for showing that science must be falsifiable and all footnotes should be read.

Kicking Science While It's Down: Paradigm Shifts and "Anything Goes"

Many people think that each scientific discovery builds upon the last one, and that science is like a big punchbowl that people in lab coats take turns spiking, to try and get everyone drunk and more amenable to hearing about their Truth.

Physicist Thomas S. Kuhn tried to show that scientific paradigms are more like rivalling fraternities waiting to push today's hot-shot paradigm off its barstool so that they can get some attention for themselves. Think of Newton's law of gravity and Einstein's law of relativity; from a distance it might seem as if Newton were almost there and that Einstein simply improved his ideas, as the calculations give the same answers most of the time. But Kuhn illustrated that the two are incommensurable (beyond comparison). For Newton, space and time were absolutes, ubiquitous and unchangeable. Einstein's relativity theory couldn't have been any more different, with space bendable and time not ticking universally but depending on mass and velocity.

Therefore, the change from one school (Newtonianism) to another (the theory of general relativity) didn't result from increasing the potency of knowledge's punch, but rather, from completely swapping one bowl for another. Kuhn even detailed examples of when inferior theories held the upper hand for some time just because they were more aesthetically appealing. Max Planck, one of the most important physics of the twentieth century, agreed: "A new scientific truth does not triumph by convincing its opponents and making them see the light, but rather because its opponents eventually die, and a new generation grows up that is familiar with it." Kuhn coined the expression "paradigm shift" to explain this.

Paul Feyerabend, a student of Karl Popper and a friend of Thomas S. Kuhn, took this idea further with his assertion that with the scientific method, as with poetry, "anything goes". Any method is just a temporary framework altered according to the needs of the community, which ultimately decides what is "scientific" and what falls short of its currently defined standards. A prominent example of this is Galileo Galilei, whose idea that the earth orbits the sun so defied scientific discourse of his day that it nearly got him executed.

Feyerabend said that theories aren't even falsified through experimentation, as Popper believed, but just fall out of fashion over time, regardless of how much evidence of their incorrectness already exists. People who hold outdated beliefs don't renounce them—they just look more and more ridiculous, stop getting invited to parties, and eventually quietly abandon them for the fashionable ones of today's "common sense". Science, like history, is written by its victors. It's not the smartest, most scientifically rigorous scientists and ideas that win, just the one's the most clout (and hard liquor) to defend their position. As Mahatma Gandhi aptly put it, "First they ignore you, then they laugh at you, then they fight you, then you win."

Science is like the comments section of the Wikipedia article about vaccination: constant edits, a lot of trolling, and no hope for a satisfactory answer everyone can agree on.

TL;DR: When it comes to science, we tend to overlook the social aspect. When it comes to social aspects, it's scientists who tend to get overlooked.

The ABC of Proving

"Imagine if there was a war and nobody showed up." The absurdity and tragic comedy of this pacifist quip stems from the fact that war is not something you have to show up for—it invades, and so is, for its participants, simply unavoidable.

Less violent but equally pervasive are new scientific discoveries. If a scientist discovers an earth-shattering insight in their field of science, they will make damn sure to distribute it quickly and get all the high fives and research funding on offer. After all, there's no Nobel Prize for best-kept secret.

Once we hit a new discovery, therefore, acceptance is only a matter of distribution, isn't it? Not so in the case of the ABC conjecture. Without getting into incomprehensible mathematical details, the story is as follows. In 2012, Shinichi Mochizuki, mathematics professor at the prestigious Kyoto University, published a paper (over five hundred pages!) claiming to have solved one of math's most fundamental problems: the ABC conjecture. If proved, it would have a ripple effect throughout all of mathematics, as many other theories would be automatically proven. For mathematicians, such proof is as elusive and desirable as a lifetime supply of ice-cream cake and school-free days are to an eight-year-old.

So far so good. The problem, unfortunately, is that the mathematics Mochizuki used to prove the conjecture is so new and complicated, that, well, nobody understands it. Which was perhaps to be expected from a paper entitled "Inter-universal Teichmüller Theory". We're not talking *Hello* magazine here.

This state of limbo has continued for several years now, to the point where even this cultured and reserved Japanese mathematician has let his frustration (just about) show: "It's a bit disappointing that no one has come out and said it's right or wrong."

Which raises the question: if nobody understands a groundbreaking truth, does it count? Truth depends on social constructs, just like everything else. Truth has to be judged by a jury of its peers, just like a defendant in a courtroom. In science, this process is called peer review. Only in this case, there are no peers with the intelligence/time/dedication to review it and declare if it's sciencey enough or not.

Which leads us to our next problem; each year machines get faster, smarter. In the future, it's likely we'll have artificial intelligence churning out new conjectures. But what's the point of that if we're simply too stupid to be able to collectively agree if the findings are correct? This isn't far-fetched; in fact, we're already there. The four-colour theorem was the first major theorem to be proven by a computer, all the way back in 1976. But because it would take millions of hours for a human to ratify it, no one has, and to this day many mathematicians are still uncomfortable accepting it as proven.

TL;DR: Scientific truths are like parties—only accepted as such if enough people show up.

Eternal Sunshine of the Paradox-Free Mind

Paradoxes are not a recent fad. They've been used to illuminate poorly understood or unsolved concepts for millennia. Theseus' ship, the barber paradox, the liar's paradox: philosophy has more paradoxes than pirates have grog. They're also really fun, if you don't have to solve them. In this seating, let's look at a few more influential brain-teasers.

The Unexpected Hanging: On a Friday, a judge tells a prisoner that he'll be hanged at noon one weekday of the following week. The day of the hanging will be a surprise. The prisoner thinks about it and concludes he will escape his hanging. How?

Well, the "surprise hanging" can't be on Friday, since if he hasn't been hanged by Thursday, it wouldn't be a surprise. But then it cannot be on Thursday either, because Friday has already been eliminated. If he has not been hung by Wednesday at noon, a Thursday hanging wouldn't be a surprise either. Using similar reasoning, he concludes that the hanging won't occur on Wednesday, Tuesday, or Monday. Problem solved.

Or . . . ? See the problem?

The prisoner doesn't, until the executioner knocks on the cell door the following Wednesday—which, despite all of the above, was an utter surprise to him. Making the judge right after all.

The Heap: You have a big heap of wheat. *Good for you.* You remove one grain from that heap. You still have a heap of wheat, correct?

You conclude that removing one single grain does not make or break a heap.

So, you keep removing grain, each time looking at your heap, until finally, you have to conclude that what you have is no longer a heap —there's just not enough grain left.

Now the problem is this: there must have been a single grain that made the difference between a heap and not a heap of wheat. If so, which one was it?

Omnipotent God: Putting aside the issue of why it would want to (personal pride, shits and giggles, etc.), can an omnipotent being create a rock too heavy for itself to lift?

If it can create such a rock, how can it be omnipotent yet fail at such a mundane task? Likewise, if it can't create such a rock, then there is a definitive limit to its powers, which violently collides with the definition of "omnipotence".

The Double-Liar Paradox. Take a piece of paper. On one side, write: "The sentence on the other side of this card is true." Turn it over, and write on the other side: "The sentence on the other side of this card is false."

See the problem?

If the second sentence is true then the first sentence is false. But if the first sentence is false, as the second sentence claims, then the second sentence would be false. Thus, both sentences are right and wrong at the same time, which is a bit like answering the question "Where was the declaration of independence signed?" with "At the bottom".

Heterological Word: A heterological word is one that does not describe itself. An example of a heterological word is "red", which is not red itself, as opposed to "polysyllabic", which is itself a polysyllabic word. So then, the next question: does "heterological" describe itself?

The Paradox of the Court: You are a lawyer. You take on a new pupil, John, with a written agreement that John will pay you back for tuition after he wins his first case. After studying, John decides to go become a dentist instead. *Not cool, John.*

So, you decide to sue John for the money he owes you. You argue that even if you lose the case, John will still have to pay you, as that would mean John had won his first case. If you win, as per the court's decision, he still must pay.

John claims that if he wins, then by the court's decision, he won't have to pay you. If, on the other hand, you win, then John would still not have won a case and would therefore not be obliged to pay.

The question is, which of the two of you is in the right and, if it's not you, how can you get revenge on John?

Next up, we'll look in detail at philosophy's most famous paradoxical race.

TL;DR: Paradoxes are the intellectual equivalent of a splinter; they seem small and inconsequential at first but get more painful and itchy the longer you look at them.

The Brain-Teaser That's Always One Step Ahead

Greek philosopher Zeno was especially well known for compiling a list of paradoxes that kept generations of philosophers confused. His most well-known paradox is Achilles and the tortoise.

Achilles and a tortoise come together for a race. Achilles, being the faster runner of the two, and a nice guy, gives the tortoise a head start. The race starts and, as expected, Achilles quickly covers that distance. During that time, however, the tortoise has advanced just a little bit further. Achilles covers that distance in the mere blink of an eye, but again, in the time that Achilles has advanced, so too has the tortoise. This, Zeno says, will keep happening repeatedly, infinite times.

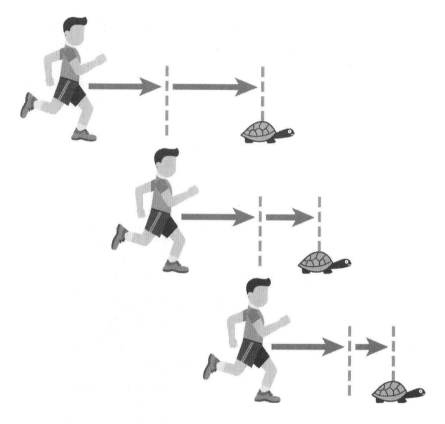

Can Achilles ever hope to overtake the slow, shelled reptile if it's always getting a little bit further away? Or do the tortoise and Lance Armstrong have the same doctor? Decide now.

Achilles does overtake the slow tortoise. Intuitively, we know this will happen. What is it that Zeno got wrong? Perhaps surprisingly, it took mathematicians two millennia to fully understand the answer. Which is way higher than the life expectancy of even the sturdiest of tortoises. The flaw is this: a process of infinite summation can still have a finite result!

The tortoise's lead is finite if Achilles is moving faster than the tortoise is. It's just a question of when Achilles will take the lead. All the paradox does is take a finite lead and begin dividing it infinitely. But dividing the lead into smaller and smaller steps isn't increasing that lead. You can keep dividing a slice of cake but it won't produce more cake. Just thinner and thinner slices of deliciousness.

To illustrate this, look at the square below, which represents the tortoise's lead. Assume that in our example, with each step from Achilles, the lead halves: $\frac{1}{2} + \frac{1}{4} + \frac{1}{8} + \ldots$ You can add infinitely more tiles within the finite area, but as the tiles keep halving, the square does not need to increase in size. The tortoise runs out of its lead, just as the series converges: $\frac{1}{2} + \frac{1}{4} + \frac{1}{8} + \ldots = 1$, at which point Achilles passes the tortoise, screaming, "Eat my dirt, reptile!"

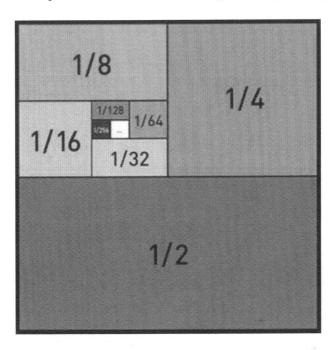

There are many other weird, brain-wrenching examples of how complicated infinity is. If you're interested, "check in" at Hilbert's hotel, or read up on the continuum hypothesis and discover that like bank accounts, some infinities are even bigger than others! You could spend forever getting to the bottom of infinity, but then that's sort of also the point.

TL;DR: Infinity isn't something to take lightly, and probably also the reason tortoises no longer take part in races.

SEATING
100

The Scientific Spectrum of Acceptable Knowledge

Isn't it strange that it's okay to be bad at some things but unacceptable to be bad at others? You can say, "I totally flunked maths at school" and get a pat on the back or acknowledging nods, but if you say, "I don't know who Shakespeare is", or "Why do meteors always land in craters?" you'll be judged more harshly.

Given that this entire book has focused on all the things worth knowing, it's somehow fitting to end it with a look at knowledge that should be avoided. Here's an overview of what you must know, what you don't have to know, and all the grey areas between.

TL;DR: If you're going to be bad at something; make it; semicolons; if you're going to be good at something, make it picking winning lottery numbers.

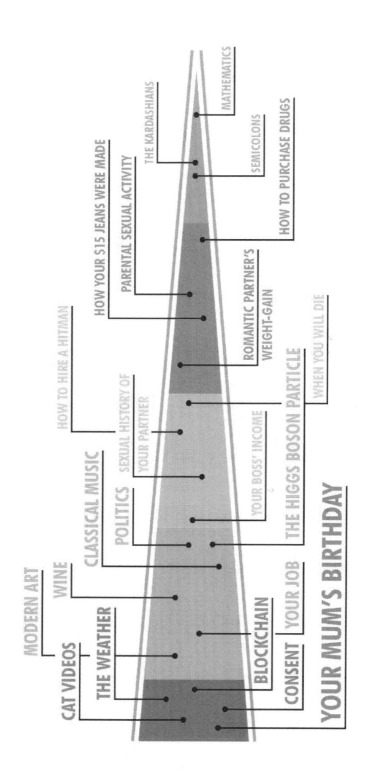

Final Exam

Are you ready to become a certified Fast Philosopher?

Fast Philosophy students, you've made it all the way to Seating 100! Congratulations on your perseverance. We've laughed, learnt, gotten equally enlightened and frustrated, and raced a turtle to infinity together. Now it's time for the final exam. Will you languish in knowledge limbo, like Schrödinger's cat? Or show your expert training, like Pavlov's dog?

Take a piece of paper and a pen. For each of the following thirty questions, note down if you think the answer is A, B, C, or D. Answers at the end. For every correct answer you'll earn one point. Get fifteen (or more) to become an official, certified *Fast* Philosopher. The last page of the book has your certificate.

If you fail, well, shame on you for not having paid enough attention. Pick up your bruised pride, return to the first chapter, and start again.

Now, we begin. Good luck!

1. Which of the following is an example of a paradox?

A: "I am always telling the truth," said the liar.

B: Only having a spoon when you just need a knife.

C: There was a deafening silence.

D: Tomorrow it will rain, or not. I'll take an umbrella anyway.

2. What is Ockham's razor for?

A: *Cleanliness.* Shaving Ockham.

B: *Precision.* Leaving no unnecessary assumption left alive in an argument.

C: *Tidiness.* Reorganising mishaps of logic.

D: *Aesthetics.* Removing the ugly parts of any explanation.

3. Which of the following is an example of Kant's a priori knowledge?

A: Knowledge that only Kant understands, e.g. pretty much all of it.

B: Knowledge that stems from experience, e.g. 27 percent of widowers killed their partners.

C: Knowledge that is contradictory to experience, e.g. the widowers' partners faked their deaths for a joke.

D: Knowledge that precedes experience, e.g. the widower's partner is dead.

4. Which philosopher would you be most likely to find, when alive, pondering his mortality in a cemetery?

A: Aristotle.

B: Martin Heidegger.

C: Marcus Aurelius.

D: Immanuel Kant.

5. I say hedonism, you say . . .

A: Diogenes of Sinope.

B: St Augustine of Hippo.

C: Epicurus.

D: Bi-curious.

6. You and I get into a heated debate about climate change. I say, "Anyone who doesn't believe in climate change must really be living on another planet." This is an example of which rhetorical fallacy?

A: Appeal to ridicule.

B: Gambler's fallacy.

C: Biased generalisation.

D: Redneck rhetoric.

7. The famous Ship of Theseus brain-teaser deals with the problem of identity because *what* happens to the ship?

A: It stops being used as a ship.

B: It's sunk by pirates.

C: All its parts are replaced one by one.

D: It is halved into two smaller ships, both called the Ship of Theseus.

8. The hermeneutic circle is . . .

A: Often faster than taking public transport.

B: The process of trying to understand a text using its whole and its individual parts.

C: The study of the meaning of ancient religious texts.

D: Not what we say but what we actually mean.

9. Which philosopher was depicted as Principal Skinner

from *The Simpsons* for his strict adherence to traditions and rules?

A: Plato.

B: Aristotle.

C: Marcus Aurelius.

D: Confucius.

10. The cheerleader effect says what?

A: People will believe anything if you tell it to them in song form.

B: The more you repeat mantras the more powerful they become.

C: Groups will naturally form around a charismatic leader.

D: People tend to appear more attractive if they're in a group.

11. Deontology says you're behaving ethical if . . .

A: The consequences of your actions are good.

B: You followed the rules.

C: You are a virtuous person (ethics will follow naturally).

D: You are always nice to small children and buy organic food.

12. How do you become more like Nietzsche's Übermensch?

A: You need a cape and an ideology.

B: You must accept that only God provides your life with meaning.

C: You must accept there is no meaning and so make your own.

D: You must move to an attic apartment.

13. What was Pascal's wager?

A: The analysis of whether it's better to believe in God or not.

B: The analysis of whether it's better to believe in one god or the other.

C: The analysis of whether it's better to believe in unicorns.

D: The analysis of whether God hates your taste in music.

14. Exegesis is . . .

A: The act of reciting religious texts.

B: The act of ignoring religious texts.

C: The act of whistling religious texts.

D: The act of interpreting religious texts.

15. "Nice car, would be a shame if something happened to it" is an example of what?

A: Hermeneutics.

B: Exegesis.

C: Indirect language.

D: Sarcasm.

16. Popper said that for science to be science it must have?

A: A published research paper.

B: Experiments.

C: Explosions and stuff.

D: Falsifiability.

17. What is the Gettier problem?

A: Can it be said that you have knowledge if there is no right answer?

B: Can it be said that you have knowledge if your beliefs are not true and justified?

C: Can it be said that you have knowledge if your reasons for believing are invalid?

D: Can it be wrong when it feels so right?

18. What did Pico della Mirandola say defines humanity?

A: Rationalism. We are it, nothing else is.

B: Purpose. We don't have it, everything else does.

C: Mortality. We know we are, nothing else does.

D: Power. If we can't have it, no one can.

19. What does Foucault mean with his "archaeology"?

A: We are all constructs of the time, the conventions, and the circumstances we live in.

B: If you dig down far enough, all people are the same.

C: Just as soil feeds plants, society serves us up its shit.

D: Just as a house has foundations, society is built on estates of knowledge.

20. According to Marx, all history can be seen as a struggle of . . .

A: Politicians.

B: Celebrities.

C: Memes.

D: Classes.

21. "Power corrupts" and "the ends justify all means" are attributed to which writer?

A: Niccolò Machiavelli.

B: Marquis de Sade.

C: Mahatma Gandhi.

D: Jean-Paul Sartre.

22. What is the main idea of Epicurean hedonism?

A: Finding pleasure in simple things.

B: Consuming as much as possible.

C: Learning to not want what everyone else has.

D: Divorcing what you love and refusing to pay it paternity.

23. What is the name of John Rawls' concept to overcome biases?

A: The original programme.

B: The original premise.

C: The unoriginal proposition.

D: The original position.

24. When do we all sign J.J. Rousseau's social contract?

A: When we become legal adults.

B: When we pay taxes.

C: When we tick the terms and conditions box.

D: Trick question. We never actually "sign" it.

25. Who rules in a plutocracy?

A: The people with the biggest guns.

B: The people with the most money.

C: The people with the most votes.

D: The people who know what "plutocracy" means.

26. What's the categorical imperative's take on the golden rule?

A: What you do to others must be in accordance with the rules of your religion.

B: What you do to others must be explainable rationally.

C: What you do to others you must wish to be a universal law.

D: What you do to others must be defensible by a good lawyer.

27. According to Plato's theory of ideas, in what way are real things represented to us?

A: As shadows on the wall.

B: As sunlight on our heads.

C: As echoes in our cave.

D: As chains on our feet.

28. According to Wittgenstein, what constitutes the limit of one's world?

A: One's language.

B: One's monetary reserves.

C: One's social contract.

D: One's passport.

29. Which of the following is not a part of Münchhausen's trilemma?

A: Infinite regression.

B: Hypothetical possibility.

C: Cyclical argument.

D: Dogmatic belief.

30. How many and what steps does the dialectic method have?

A: One: Direction.

B: Two: Yourself and the antagonist.

C: Three: Question, answer, rebuttal.

D: Four: The thesis, the antithesis, crisis, and the resulting synthesis.

* * *

Answers: 1 A, 2 B, 3 D, 4 B, 5 C, 6 A, 7 C, 8 B, 9 D, 10 D, 11 B, 12 C, 13 A, 14 D, 15 C, 16 D, 17 C, 18 B, 19 A, 20 D, 21 A, 22 A, 23 D, 24 B, 25 B, 26 C, 27 A, 28 A, 29 B, 30 D

FAST PHILOSOPHY

CERTIFICATE

Fast Philosophy School certifies that

_____

has successfully completed the course in Philosophy,

With _____ points they are now officially qualified to use the title of

FAST PHILOSOPHER

№ 90479

Adam Fletcher
PRESIDENT

Lukas N.P. Egger
FACULTY DIRECTOR

Help me keep doing this

You made it all the way to the end? Fantastic. Thank you. You're a wonderful human. We'm extremely grateful you took a chance on Lukas and I (there's a song in that, we think).

Want to know the hardest part of being a writer? It's not the words —it's everything that happens after the words. We don't have a publisher supporting this book. We don't have a big marketing budget to help people find it. We can't put up posters of my face in the subway. We can't hire a blimp to circle the Super Bowl.

But we have something much more powerful and effective anyway, something publishers would kill for—**a group of loyal readers**. Readers like you. Honest reviews work like rocket fuel for books. Writing a review is the best thing you can do to both thank us and help other people find our books. We want there to be more books. We hope you do too. Please consider leaving a review on Amazon or wherever you got this book. It makes all the difference.

Thank you. We owe you.

Adam and Lukas

Also by Adam Fletcher: Don't Go There

How much would you risk to change your life? Would you go where everyone else is trying to leave?

Best-selling author Adam Fletcher must ,there's something he wants to know. Something no-one is telling. To get the answer he'll have to go to some of the strangest places in the world: North Korea, Chernobyl, Transnistria, Liberland, and many more. On a quest that will threaten his sanity, safety and relationship to his eccentric German girlfriend, Annett.

Why will he enter a blizzard with only a pack of biscuits? Why will the Croatian police chase him down the Danube? What does the Devil incarnate tell him on a bus in Moldova? Will it all be worth it? Will he make it back home? Will anyone be waiting when he does?

Find out in Don't Go There: the best-selling, hilarious travel memoir full of **unusual characters, crazy destinations, and British humour.**

The British are not who they think they are! Come on a hilarious tour of the most misunderstood people on Earth. Throwing away all the usual, boring stereotypes, Adam Fletcher will explain:

- What cricket has to do with the Grim Reaper.

- When you shouldn't say sorry.

- The real reason Brexit happened.

- Which secret religion every Brit is a member of.

- The Ten Commandments of British humour.

And much more. The truth about the British will surprise you. Discover it now!

Manufactured by Amazon.ca
Bolton, ON

22225574R00157